Jochen Erler

The Telegram to Stalin
A Political Memoir of My Life in Three Germanys

Jochen Erler

The Telegram to Stalin
A Political Memoir of My Life
in Three Germanys

This is the self-published English version of Jahrgang'32, Dreimal Deutsche Beschattung, Politische Memoiren, ISBN-10: 0578421208, and ISBN-13: 978-0578421209. Originally published in 2006 by edition Lithaus in Berlin, and available through Amazon and other retail outlets, it has been translated by Lynn Erler, revised by Katherine Bodner, Cordelia Hebblethwaite and designed by Merlin T. Lee of Wizigns.

Table of Contents

SINCE 1956

IN THE WEST

EPILOGUE

Foreword

In this remarkable book Jochen Erler describes the history of his family and his life, passing through three political regimes during an epoch of radical social change in Germany.

Erler vividly portrays in *The Telegram to Stalin* the persecution and discrimination he experienced himself under three political systems. His will for self-assertion and courage is apparently an inherited Erler family trait: his father was once expelled from the Nazi Party because he neither used the Hitler salute, nor participated in the defamation of the Jewish population. Jochen followed his father on the path of civil insubordination and suspiciousness of all ideologies and simplistic concepts of an enemy; the responses of one's own conscience are more important than collective and transitory trends and slogans.

The author takes us along on his journey from the last years of the war to postwar Germany: his adventures in the Soviet Occupation Zone and persecution by the Communists due to a harmless leaflet, being sentenced and imprisoned in Bautzen, his escape to Federal Germany, and how he faced new complications and problems in the "Golden West", even in diplomatic circles. The author's bitter lessons and insight are sobering and instructive at the same time.

Jochen Erler proves himself a reliable witness and chronicler of a century full of radical historic change and social catastrophe. However, he does not give up, but courageously stands up for human rights and justice; he remains true to his principles to today and is committed - among other forums - to the German League for Human Rights.

Jochen Erler's book deserves a wide audience. It is especially recommended to readers of the young generation.

Friedrich Nolte, Secretary General of the German League for Human Rights (translated by J. Erler)

1932-1945
THE BROWN YEARS

CHILDHOOD IN HITLER'S GERMANY

What Father Taught Me

My father was my hero and role model. He was a freethinker and a Mason, a liberal with no respect for authority imposed without legitimacy. During Hitler's regime on workers' memorial day on 1 May he wore a red carnation in his lapel. This was the symbol of the Socialists and Communists, whose political parties had been outlawed. After just a few years as a member of Hitler's party he was thrown out because he refused to give the Nazi salute Heil Hitler or to participate in the persecution of Jews. In the beginning, he admitted that he had been impressed, like the great majority of Germans, by Hitler's ability to put an end to the disastrous wrangle of more than 30 political parties.

My father was completely unencumbered by pedagogical thinking - or I should say by the established theories of how to instill correct behaviour in children. Instead he taught us children - we were three brothers - to accept authority only if its rules are just and reasonable, and to distance ourselves from established norms which do not meet this criterion. Father encouraged us to question the decisions our nanny made, and to engage in challenging discussions at the dinner table. Father often admitted that we children were in the right when issues arose due to the inflexibility of the nanny.

At our cottage in Falkenhain in the nearby mountains, we spent many weekends and some school vacations together with our beloved cook and without the nanny - who thankfully went to her family home. My father initiated the maxim "Everything is allowed in Falkenhain." In our cottage we could ignore the established manners that were drilled into us at home in Dresden.

3

We could slurp our soup, eat with our elbows on the table and lie around on a bench after a meal. We could wear old clothes or even run around without any. We were liberated of any need to follow manners that we saw as a straightjacket imposed by society. Near limitless freedom reigned in our weekend house - but only there. When we were in hotels at the North Sea coast or at the Millsttätter Lake in Austria, we behaved well according to the established norms - and we did this without any misgivings.

During the war years of 1939-45, petrol became scarce and family trips in our Opel Kapitän were no longer allowed by the authorities. The car was requisitioned anyhow. So my father drove his Ford Eifel delivery van to Falkenhain, declaring his journeys as "business trips". At every control point on the road, we children had to hide under a blanket in the goods area of the van. We also made what we called hamster trips scurrying out to Bohemia where my father knew he could get butter and the occasional goose. These purchases could not have been completely legal because the items were carefully hidden every time we came within sight of a road control point.

We developed an admiration for our father as a heroic warrior against the Nazi authorities. Two incidents describe why. The first occurred during the winter seasonal fundraising for the war, the so called *Winterhilfswerk*, when Nazi commissioned representatives went around town like travelling salesmen from shop to shop to sell overpriced postcards and other items that were blatant Nazi propaganda. Our father owned and ran, together with my mother prior to their divorce, the interior decorating department store Gardinen Erler on Ferdinand Street in the centre of Dresden. At the time it was the leading store for interior decoration in town. One day, a man from the *Winterhilfswerk* entered my father's store and began to bother customers. My father grabbed him by the collar and put him out on the street with the admonition "We don't need your

4

My father's store for interior decoration, located near the Prager Strasse, had two floors for shopping and a third floor for sewing staff.

garbage here." Thanks to his contacts my father got away with only a warning from the authorities.

I can still see the second incident before me, which occurred at the cottage in Falkenhain, as if it were yesterday. We always hoisted our family flag: three white hearts on a red background, to signal to our friends who were on their way from Dresden to their cottages in nearby Waldidylle or Oberbärenburg that we were in residence. From our cottage on the south side of the hill we could see the main road in the valley with its sporadic traffic. One weekend, when we were lounging in sun chairs or playing on the meadow, we saw an open top Mercedes with SA officers stop on the road while the officers looked about. They turned around and drove up to our house.

The brownshirts were angry because on Hitler's birthday, 20 April, we were not displaying the swastika flag as required by

Our beloved weekend house in Falkenhain in the Erzgebirge Mountains was a steady element of family life. We lived here after the bombardment of Dresden, and experienced the last weeks of Hitler's regime here. Some people in our village claimed we would give light signals to the Anglo-American bomber squadrons.

law. My father smoothly explained that the permission he had been granted from the authorities to fly his own flag was an overriding special rule - *lex specialis derogat lex generalis*. The heated exchange that followed culminated with one officer losing control entirely, shouting at my father and threatening to arrest him. My father stood his ground. In any case he didn't even have a Hakenkreuz flag! As a consequence, my father's right to fly a personal flag was withdrawn, and he got an official reprimand. His friends in high place warned him seriously and urgently not to provoke another conflict with the authorities as they would be unable to shield him from the concentration camps for a third time.

What a hero our dad was for us! We knew something of arrests, deportation and concentration camps because we listened regularly to BBC radio broadcasts from London. I will never forget the voice of Lindley Fraser, the broadcaster on BBC's German programme. As the Russians came ever closer we also began to listen to Radio Moscow's German language programme.

You would be punished severely if you were caught listening to enemy broadcasts. We had an upmarket Blaupunkt radio that picked up BBC and Radio Moscow. On the mass-produced radio, broadcasting frequences were controlled so only German radio stations were available. This *Volksempfänger* was colloquially named *Göbbelsschnauze* (Goebbels's snout) after the Minister for propaganda.

Later, under the communist regime in Eastern Germany, my father continued his oppositional stance towards the authorities but was not quite so provocative about it. He had to be more careful because he no longer had contacts in circles of power. Nevertheless, while party members and functionaries of the regime wore a red carnation in their lapels on 1 May, my dad proudly promenaded through town with a yellow flower on his coat, symbolising the liberals. Political jokes were shared amongst friends and he could not resist making ironic comments in public - either on the street or in the tram - whenever he saw political slogans on banners or posters. This could have been interpreted as *Boykotthetze*, boycott agitation, against the Deutsche Demokratische Republik (DDR) according to Article 6 of the constitution. Yet the authorities appeared to be content to leave the old man alone.

On the other hand the tax authorities conducted a *Tiefen-prüfung* (an in-depth audit) and applied a retroactive income tax designed to expropriate the few remaining privately owned businesses. They dispossessed him. His shop was taken in lieu of supposed tax dereliction and was closed. He could not pay the taxes - which even under DDR laws were illegal.

None of this passed me by without leaving a mark. I also developed a suspicion for civil authorities, especially in Eastern Germany where personal freedom in many respects was not respected. I felt a kind of thrill when defying the higher-ups. But I did not get away with it as lightly as my father did.

Life Under the Nazis

Dresden

Service as a *Pimpf* - the lowest rank of the *Hitlerjugend* (HJ), the Nazi Youth movement - was not to my liking and I often avoided participating in their activities. My *Jungenschaft* (the youngest level of HJ) met every week near St Luke's church and was led by my friend Fritz Oschatz as our *Jungenschaftführer*, the leader of our unit. Together with the other Jugenschaften of our *Fähnlein* 53, the next level in the HJ's hierarchy, we had to do body strengthening exercises, and most importantly to learn songs and to march. I preferred to spend my weekends in our weekend house in the mountains outside Dresden. The paramilitary drills and activities were not to my liking. After several warnings due to multiple absences, I was punished with several days of house arrest, which I had to spend sitting in a locked room in the apartment of our *Stammführer*, the leader of the regional HJ in Dresden.

When one of my friends from the Gutzkow street primary school was given the yellow Star of David, the *Judenstern*, because his parents were Jews, I was counselled to break off any communication with him. Nevertheless we met up from time to time, secretly. One day my friend and his family simply disappeared. I never found out whether they had emigrated or been put to a concentration camp.

Wendisch-Baselitz

In 1943, all children were evacuated from Dresden because there was a high risk of Allied bombing. My older brother and I were sent to the farm of the Schmoles, a family my father knew in Wendisch-Baselitz. The Wendish people are a homogenous minority within Germany who kept their Slavic language, local customs and traditional dress thanks to a certain degree of autonomy that was respected by Hitler and later by the communist regime. Deeply rooted in Catholicism, the Wendish people of Saxony never aligned themselves with Hitler. They treated prisoners of war and people from occupied territories (called *DPs* after the war, *displaced persons*) who had to work on their farms, exactly the same way as ordinary farm labourers.

My brother and I didn't hide our sympathy for the Wendish people, for the foreigners, or our disapproval of the Hitler regime. We stood guard whenever Radio Moscow or BBC London was tuned in and smuggled messages between the farm and a prisoner of war camp near Kamenz, where there was a shoe factory manned by prisoners of war and *DPs*. My 14-year-old brother and I aged 11 years were never suspected by the guards at the camp entrances.

On the farm I made a special friendship with a French prisoner of war named Emile, who had his own farm back in Normandy. Emile said that after the war I could come with him as I wasn't a *boche* - the derogatory French term for a German. He anticipated the years of hunger that were to follow the destruction of Germany. I was proud to have him as a future protector and truly had in mind going with him to France once the war ended. Fate separated us though. It is doubtful I would have abandoned my family in the difficult postwar years, and in any case they would not have allowed me to leave.

In Wendisch-Baselitz, my older brother and I managed to stay clear of the local HJ that marched in step with music and flags through the village every Sunday. I spent my free time instead with my school friends Klaus Hossenfelder and Siegfried Strieter in a nearby quarry. In our youthful exuberance and ignorance we adopted the name *Chicago Gangsters*. Our emblem was a skyscraper with the flag of Illinois. America was our dream!

But one day the local Nazi leader from neighbouring Nebelschütz - Wendisch-Baselitz had no area leader - arrived at the Schmoles's farm, proud in his full SA uniform, and made a right fuss about our absence from the HJ service. We pleaded ignorance, although we knew full well that membership and attendance of activities was obligatory for all school-aged children, and gave the excuse that we had not received an order to attend. We feared we would be put under youth arrest but fortunately we got away with just a warning. From then on we had to appear for service every Sunday.

At the prestigious Lessing School in Kamenz, about 7 km from Wendisch-Baselitz, that we attended, my brother Klaus made friends with a classmate from Nebelschütz. The latter's father had been arrested as a communist and condemned to a concentration camp. The two boys revealed to me their plan to steal explosives from one of the many local quarries where dynamite and ignition materials were stored in a small storage cave. They asked me to join. Their intention was to blow up bridges as the war was coming to an end and thus to sabotage German troop movements. One night we set out with a handcart, broke open the lock of the storeroom and brought our loot to our friend's house where he hid it in empty beehives. The break-in at the explosive depot had been reported to the police and the imprint of the wheels of our handcart had been traced to the house of our friend, so the three of us were placed under police observation though we were unaware of it at the time.

11

Another event accelerated our downfall. My brother experimented in one the rooms at the Schmoles with small quantities of black powder he had removed from some stolen hunting cartridges. With youthful enthusiasm he wanted to build landmines following a description that he had found in a military technical magazine. However one night there was an explosion with an accompanying flash of light. The inner wall of our room lay in rubble and ash and the curtains had caught fire. During an electric blackout Klaus had been working by candlelight. He was lucky to lose just one finger.

As a consequence of this event and the break-in, we lost the freedom we enjoyed in the countryside. Klaus was sent to a Nazi run boarding institution for young delinquents, a *Straf-NAPO-LA* (Penal National Political Institute of Education), and I went to a boarding school for maladjusted youth in Altenberg with institutionalised paramilitary drills. Our friend was placed under youth arrest.

Altenberg

At the Altenberg boarding school I met a lot of similar thinking young people who disliked the regime and its propaganda and training. When there was no teacher nearby, we exchanged political jokes. During morning assembly we had to raise our arm while singing Nazi songs. We would be in the back rows where our school director in Nazi uniform could not hear us. We sang our own text with the melody of the SA song "Es zittern die morschen Knochen" (brittle bones are shaking ...). Our text began with the same words, but we replaced the rest with our own anti-Hitler rhymes.

As the end of the war approached - at the end of 1944, early 1945 - food became scarcer and we boys were hungry. All food was rationed, with the exception of fruit and vegetables for which we had to stand in queues. There were red cards for bread, which had two different vouchers, each gave permission to buy 750g of bread. One voucher had a black stripe across it and the other said *oder 500g Mehl* (500g flour) on it. There must have been a shortage of flour because the vouchers also permitting the purchase of flour had been declared invalid. We boys had a great idea: to create falsified bread vouchers. We collected the invalid vouchers and changed the *oder 500g Mehl* to a black stripe with black ink. For a good number of weeks we were able to procure enough bread to be able to trade some for other foodstuffs.

However, soon the source of invalid coupons dried up and we had to think of new ways to deal with our hunger. In time-honoured fashion, while one boy engaged the market tradesmen in conversation we stole potatoes - by now also rationed. We had plenty of good opportunities to roast our potatoes out in the open over a wood fire. Almost daily there was an air attack alarm and instead of running to the shelter, a disused quarry in the middle of Altenberg, our clique ran out to open fields. We hated the damp, cold shelter. We could see the formation of the American flying fortresses. We quoted Herman Göring's boasting at the beginning of the war with sarcasm: "Call me plain Meier if ever an enemy aircraft trespasses into German airspace" - he was of course called "Hermann Meier" by us.

The Night Dresden was Bombed

During the course of our many escapades I got to know a soldier who was stationed at an observation post on a hillside just 10 minutes away from our school. He introduced me to the tactical principles of air combat as occasionally we could observe such action when the German Messerschmitts ME109 attacked the flying fortresses. But soon the American bombers

13

My father stands in front of our house after the bombing raid of Dresden on 13 February 1945.

passed unhindered through German airspace.

On my hometown Dresden's fatal night of 13 February 1945 I was at the observation post instead of in the shelter. I could see in the far distance light markers drifting on their little parachutes, called Christmas trees. They were positioned above Dresden. It was an impressive and fascinating air show. I quipped to the soldier there: "Isn't it fantastic?" His answer was unforgettable: "This is a death sentence for Dresden." I shuddered and had nothing to say. My father always stayed late into the evening in his store in the centre of Dresden. My mother, who had separated, lived in Berlin. So far she had survived the bombings there. What would happen to him? Soon the searchlights beamed into the sky, but there was no sound of anti-aircraft guns. All the anti-aircraft artillery had been sent from Dresden to the Eastern Front to fight the Russian T-34 tanks. Soon the burning of the city began. I watched the inferno.

Two hours later there were more air raid alarms. I was still at the observation post so as not to miss any of the terrible sight. This time double-rump bombers flew at low-altitude above us- there was some light from the moon and not many clouds. With field glasses I could see how the bellies of the bombers opened and how the bombs of the second attack fell on the burning city. This systematic method of destruction was called carpet bombing. We wondered where our fighter planes were... None ever did arrive.

The next day there was no school. We had to help prepare emergency shelters in all available public buildings of Altenberg: the train station, sports hall and town hall. Soon the first trains arrived. The survivors were hungry, tired and smelled strongly of fire. Train after train came, amongst them the *Fliegender Hamburger* (Flying Hamburger), a modern fast train that normally ran between Hamburg and Dresden. The escapees had to sleep on straw like herrings. Doctors and nurses were busy day and night. So were we boys.

We heard terrible stories. The heat of the fire in the city centre had melted the asphalt of the streets and it had even caught fire. Water in the public fountains where people had looked for protection had boiled. One of the bombers had shot into the crowds of people who had fled to the *Großer Garten*, the great park not far from the railway station. Some of the animals of Dresden's Zoological Garden, which was located in the park, had run wild and among them a lion who reportedly settled to sleep among the people. Huge bombs had burned holes in brick walls like flamethrowers. Against this there was no defence. Dresden residents, like all citizens of big cities, had been trained how to extinguish fires caused by phosphor sticks. Facing the unexpected fire in Dresden, covering burning fire sticks seemed like child's play.

Some days later, school resumed but in the afternoons we had to do military training. Hitler needed cannon fodder - children and the elderly were called to arms. As a 13-year-old, I was trained to handle a heavy machine gun, which was so heavy I could not lift it. Fortunately I never had to use it. The cannons were thundering in neighbouring Bohemia: the Russians were at the gates of Prague and near the German border.

Shortly before the Altenberg school closed, I became the focus of attention, thanks to my beloved Falkenhain. In the middle of a lesson, I was called out of the classroom by two Gestapo officials (Geheime Staatspolizei, the Secret Police) dressed in civilian clothes and ready to interrogate me. It turned out that our family was suspected of making flashing light signals from our weekend house to Allied airplanes! What a crazy idea! I could explain the lights. After having lost everything in the Dresden bombings, my parents had moved to Falkenhain where our former cook and now our nanny had been taking care of my younger brother Frido who went to school there. Although our weekend house had the required blackout windows at night, we hadn't blacked out the one small window in the attic where we slept under the eaves. There was no electric light, and we used a flashlight powered by a dynamo when we climbed up the ladder to our attic bedroom furnished with mattresses on its floor. Those were the so-called light signals that had been seen by people in the village and denounced to the authorities.

My boarding school in Altenberg closed and we children were sent home. I packed my rucksack, took my bike and went to our weekend house in nearby Falkenhain where both my father and mother, who had returned from Berlin, together with my two brothers, were waiting for me.

This well and trough were our place for washing and bathing, because our weekend house at the border of the forest was not connected to the village water supply.

Falkenhain

I spent the last weeks of the war in Falkenhain. Our idyllic weekend cottage had become, in the meantime, something of a refugee camp. Family friends who had also been bombed out of Dresden had sought and gained temporary accommodation with us. There wasn't space for everyone to sleep inside the small house. We built two shelters in the woods above our cottage with felled fir logs that had been prepared for shipment. So we had ample space for our "guests" to sleep. But during the daytime, our small cottage was crowded. We collected water from a forest spring and our bathtub was an outdoor wooden tub. We had a pit toilet only.

From what I remember, though, life was harmonious even though food portions were getting ever smaller. We began to barter useful items we had for potatoes and grain from the farmers. We collected herbs from the meadows and fields to make salads, soups and tea.

On clear days the airplanes provided entertainment and excitement. We could watch the huge American bombers with their white contrails. They were rarely engaged by our Messerschmitts. If they were, though, once in a while a shot out or burning flying fortress would come spiraling down. When the parachutes came down in our area, we were supposed to find the "bad Americans" and notify the authorities. My father and we three boys separated ourselves from the rest of the villagers who might be out looking and shouted in English "Watch out! Keep in hiding! The village people are after you." I spent my pre-sleep dreams imagining I had found a pilot and was helping him to safety...

The very low-altitude flying small Russian planes were dangerous. We watched them as they flew above our valley shooting into the lines of refugees who were walking only 250 yards away on our country road. The German military was using the main roads in the valley and not the smaller country and mountain roads where the refugees were streaming toward the West to escape from the Russians.

Deserting German soldiers often came by our cottage as it lies close to the edge of the forest. They asked for civilian clothes and we helped where we could. In the forest we boys found all sorts of discarded weapons that we then played with. We encountered two brand-new armour-plated scout cars. The starters worked, but the tanks were empty. My older brother dismantled the radio installations and built two radios out of the recuperated gear. We threw away the collected pistols and machine guns, thank goodness. If the Russians, who arrived later, had found weapons in our possession we would have been treated as *Werwölfe* (partisans) and condemned to at least twenty five years of hard labour, as it happened with some other youngsters that I later met in prison.

1945-1956
THE RED YEARS

UNDER THE COMMUNISTS

The Soviet Troops

We boys were actually disappointed when the Red Army finally marched into Falkenhain. Instead of threatening T-34 tanks and *Stalinorgeln* (artillery which caused frightening noises), Mongolian troops came in with *Panjewagen*, wagons similar to those used to go West in the US pulled by tangle haired ponies. We asked ourselves how our army could have been defeated by these hordes of wild men. Later we found out that these were only the occupation troops. The modern fighting units were put, right after the armistice, in army barracks where they were isolated from any contact with the German population. Only the support units destined to take control of the occupied villages and towns could enjoy their roles as winners of the war: they plundered houses and farms, raped women, went hunting deer at night with cars they had requisitioned. However, the occupation troops paid a high price for having had contact with a higher standard of life than at home. After a few months when new local governments were formed, instead of being repatriated to their families back home, Stalin sent them all to Siberian forced labour camps to silence them. Only those troops who had been restricted to army barracks were allowed to see their families again.

The soldiers treated us like the village poor. We lived in a modest overcrowded little wooden cottage with about ten friends who had been bombed out in Dresden and had no other place to find shelter. In contrast our neighbours - artisans and forest workers - had attractive individual family homes, built under Hitler's rule. Soldiers gave us things they had

21

stolen there. We were advised to hide our second bicycle because under communist rule only one bicycle was allowed per family. Having two bicycles was deemed capitalistic excess! This gave us our first insight into the Soviet ideology so frequently advanced by the Communists on the radio and in the press.

The officer in our village who had the highest rank gave himself the title *Kommandant*, Commander, and became lord and master over us. He commanded all farm animals and had them driven together into the largest farmyard of our village where he resided. He named the farm his commander's post. Since the cows had to be milked, the people of our village were allowed onto the farm. So we at least got milk!

The soldiers gave us children chocolate and Allied money. One of them ventured to say, "Hitler shit, Stalin shit." We wondered whether this remark stemmed from the higher standard of living they found in Germany. For instance they had never seen taps or toilets. "Water out of the wall" was what they called it. They even accused a house owner of theft because the potatoes they had been washing in the toilet had disappeared. We found out later that Russians had made holes one above the other in the floors of houses with several stories in order to build a latrine and used the cellar as a cesspit. Or was Stalin really not much better than Hitler in the eyes of these Russians?

Only Three Years of Relative Freedom

Dresden

After my family's return to Dresden, to its southern suburb, I went to the high school in Dresden Plauen. We lived as unwelcomed subtenants in a single-family house unaffected by the bombing. It was a rule that non-bombed residents were obliged to take-in bombed-out victims as subtenants.

During the first three years after liberation from Nazi rule, we found Stalin's policies for the SBZ, the Soviet Occupation Zone, not bad at all. Free parties were created that published their own, admittedly censored, newspapers. We could even subscribe to the *Jugendtelegraph*, the voice of the young Social Democrats published in West Berlin.

In school, pupil and parent councils were constituted following free elections. Student councils were elected to have a consultative role in the running of the universities. Factory workers and employees were also allowed representative councils. These groups were all tools of democratisation never experienced under Hitler.

I joined the Liberal Democratic Party (LDP) at sixteen and attended a weekend seminar in the district party school in Radebeul near Dresden where the lecturers explained the goals of our party. I was also one of the first members of the Association for German-Soviet Friendship in Dresden. This institution fostered the dissemination of Russian culture, music, literature, and also of communist ideology. However, the saying "Children, enjoy the war because peace will be terrible" certainly

In 1947, I was 15 years of age. Before the start of the red terror, I still believed in German-Soviet friendship.

proved itself: we suffered near starvation. What was in normal times fed to the pigs was a delicacy for us. Whey enhanced with aroma and saccharin was a delicious drink. A nutritious spread was made out of the leftovers of pressed oilseed rape with some vinegar and herbs. We ate yeast flakes made from sawdust. We made trips into the countryside and exchanged whatever items we could spare for food.

Satirical commentators said that the farmers were fitting their cowsheds with carpets. We learned how to cook nettles as spinach and collected many plants to make salad and soups. In the autumn we collected mushrooms. Our efforts in the fields after harvest were tediously difficult but rewarding as after a heavy rain we found potatoes that had been overlooked, or we plucked ears from a field where the grain had been harvested. We ground the rye or wheat in a hand turned mill.

Hermann-Lietz-Schule Haubinda

Day after day, our parents had to try to quell the hunger of three adolescent boys. Eventually it was no longer possible as there simply was not enough food to be found and our parents had no more personal belongings they could barter. So they sent us to boarding schools that had their own farms.

I went to the Hermann-Lietz School in Haubinda in the district of Hildburghausen in Thuringia. It belonged to a Foun-

24

dation created by Hermann Lietz, a pedagogue whose ideas were close to those of Pestalozzi. In the morning, we performed schoolwork for the brain, in the afternoon work for the hands: farm, forest, and carpentry. I opted for forestry. Regarding discipline and physical education, it was not much different from the Nazi-orientated school I had attended in Altenberg. To prove our heartiness in Altenberg we had to dive headfirst from the 10 metre high diving board into the pool, and in winter we had to master the ski-jump at the Galgenberg resulting in a jump of at least 7 m distance. In Haubinda we had to harden ourselves by running barefoot in the early morning over gravel, in only our swimming costumes, and then through a frosty meadow to the swimming pool, swim and then run back to the house dripping wet.

On the other hand, my stomach got filled, if only for a short while because soon the authorities closed down the older classes at the school. The reason for this was that senior students regularly crossed the *green border* into Coburg in the American occupied zone. This was forbidden. At that time the border separating the Soviet occupation zone from the Western zones in Germany was only lightly patrolled and we boys knew enough secret ways through the forest to get to promising Coburg where we could find rare goods in the shops. Later on when the borders were made more secure, the school had to close down completely because it was in the newly created no-man's land along the border between West and East Germany. This border later was called *Todeszone* (death zone) because the East German border guards had been instructed to shoot at refugees trying to cross the border, like at the Berlin Wall.

The Iron Curtain

When Jan Masaryk, the minister of foreign affairs of the free-ly elected Government of Czechoslovakia, was killed in Prague - according to the authorities he committed suicide by jump-ing out of a window, a claim nobody believed - and when a se-ries of political show trials in Soviet-controlled countries took place in 1948, an icy wind began to blow from the East. Vir-tually all democratic achievements from the years 1945-1948 were brought under communist control. The only youth organ-isation that was permitted was the communist-leaning *Freie Deutsche Jugend* (FDJ) whose chairman was Erich Honecker, the future President of the future *Deutsche Demokratische Republik* (DDR). There were no more *Falken* (Young Socialists) or *Junge Union* (Young Christian Union) or *Jungliberale* (Young Liberals).

The *SPD* (Social Democratic Party) had to fuse with the *KPD* (Communist Party) - the latter had received only 15-20% of the vote in free elections - to form the *SED* (Sozialistische Ein-heitspartei) where the Communists obtained control. The other political parties remained officially independent but were sub-sumed within the *National Front* and brought under Mos- cow's control. Anyone holding an official post who tried to maintain his independence and integrity had to step down or was in-dicted and charged as a "lackey of the West". On election day, there were lists of candidates of the *National Front* instead of different lists for candidates of the various political parties. "Ob ja, ob nein, es wird dasselbe sein" (whether yes or no, the result will be the same) was a well known hit tune that Radio Leipzig broadcasted on election day in 1949. This bit of irony was paid for by the person responsible. She lost her job and fled to West Berlin where she got a job with *RIAS* (Radio in the American Sector of Berlin).

FDJ demonstrations: to be admitted to the final exams at high school, all students had to join the official youth movement (FDJ) and to be politically active. I became responsible for cultural affairs in the FDJ Committee of our district and had to participate in many demonstrations. Among the members of the FDJ were many informers of the Stasi.

(Centre) Russian soldiers watching.

Political pressure increased year on year. Interaction across occupied zones in Germany became more and more difficult. The four sectors inside Berlin were the exceptions: the sector occupied by the Russians in the Eastern part of Berlin and the three Western sectors occupied by the Americans, English and French. The Soviet Secret Service (NKWD) and East Germany's Secret Police Department, which later became the *Staatssicherheitsdienst* (Stasi) developed a thick network of spies and denouncers in East Germany.

There were arrests on political grounds. In the schools ideological brainwashing was the order of the day but most students remained unconvinced. We listened to the broadcasts of RIAS and BBC and secretly passed around newspapers from the West. We could see through the communist propaganda and categorically rejected Stalinist terror as well as his personality cult.

Black Marketeering

Black markeering played a big role in our lives. We probably couldn't have survived the post-war era without it. I managed a lucrative black market business in our neighbourhood. Sometimes my older brother in West Berlin helped me to get the merchandise that was not available in the East. He had been denied access to university in East Germany because he was, like myself, the son of a despised "capitalist" merchant. He had gone for that

Father with us three brothers

28

reason to West Berlin in order to study at the *Freie Universität* (Free University). My cash flow was better than my parents' who had reopened a store under the old name of *Gardinen Erler, Haus für Mode und Heimkunst* (Curtain/ Draperies Erler, Fashion and Interior Decorating). They often had to borrow money from me.

My best-selling merchandise was fruit liqueur. A friend of mine, Fred Schellenberger, a chemistry student who lived in our neighbourhood, had invented a method of distilling perfectly clean ethyl alcohol from *Brennspiritus* (denatured spirit) by eliminating the bitter tasting components. I provided Fred with gallons of Brennspiritus from my uncle Heinz Plietzsch, owner of a business producing and repairing boilers and other metal vessels. Brennspiritus was otherwise not available, even on the black market. In return, my uncle received our home-made liqueur: ethyl alcohol sweetened with sugar and flavoured with fruit aromas, or made as *Magenbitters* (bitters) with easily obtainable herbs. As Fred's parents lived abroad, because his father was a professor at the university in Greifswald, we had a perfect place for undisturbed distilling. Although the stairwell leading to Fred's apartment smelled like a distillery, surprisingly no tenant of the house ever denounced our obviously illegal activity.

The profit from my black market dealings permitted me to install a laboratory for chemical experiments in my room. At school I was an assistant to the teacher in Chemistry and my ambition was to become a patent lawyer. However, while conducting an experiment, I caused an explosion, which was so bad that I lost one eye and several fingers on my right hand.

Black market activities intensified in the East after the 1948 currency reforms, which took place in both parts of Germany. Suddenly there were shops full of goods in the western sectors while in the East we still lacked everyday items, in particular

29

imported wares like coffee, cigarettes, citrus fruits, chocolate, nylon tights, condoms and so forth. This affected the exchange rate between the two currencies. Most of the time until re-unification in 1989, one Westmark bought four Eastmarks.

My assortment of goods included high-quality sewing machine needles for export to Poland where they were used for the production of handguns. I traded cigarettes, groceries and condoms. One day on my way back from a shopping trip in West Berlin, I had two wooden crates of smoked herring with me. The whole tram smelt of them and under pressure from fellow passengers, I sold all the fish to them.

In another incident I overheard my mother speaking over the telephone to a friend about some quality hand soap she had found for sale under the counter in a nearby government shop (*Handels Organisation*, HO). I told my mother that her friend could get the same soap cheaper from me as I was the one who had supplied it to the sales clerk at the HO shop.

I was known as a black market dealer at school as well. Even teachers came to me for goods. Our English teacher Dr Kaden and our fabulous maths teacher Mr Knebel were regular customers of mine for bread and cigarettes. My classmates noticed this of course and urged me to make my deliveries conditional on the teachers telling stories from their youth and career. I only gently pressed these teachers, but I have to say those few hours created an excellent relationship between the teachers and us.

I eventually found out from an acquaintance that black marketing was also a Russian "weapon" during the cold war, which few people knew. This acquaintance, named Friedel, worked as a chemist in the half destroyed buildings of the old cigarette factory in Dresden. He was responsible for the production of fake *Lucky Strike, Chesterfield and Pall Mall* cigarettes, which the Russians put on the black market to get hard currency at a time when Dollars and Westmarks were parallel currencies in East Germany. Friedel was the only person I knew in my wide circle of acquaintances who had the permission to travel abroad and to possess foreign currency. He had to buy tobacco on the international market to enable him to produce cigarettes that tasted the same as those he copied. There were rumours that like the cigarettes made in Dresden, *Cadbury Chocolate* was being produced in Czechoslovakia primarily for the black market in West Berlin.

Summer 1949 in the schoolyard of my high school in Dresden-Plauen, my nickname was Rano.

West Berlin and the Investigations Committee of Freedom Lawyers

I often took the train to East Berlin and continued unhindered into West Berlin where my older brother Klaus studied at the *Freie Universität*. I had the opportunity to explore cultural life in the free sectors of the city and remember especially some of the films, particularly the French film *Manon*, and also the political cabaret *Die Stachelschweine* which I saw with my brother.

I enjoyed the *Kunilogenrummel*, a piece of fun by the students of the *Freie Universität* in West Berlin where they had jokingly convinced Jakob Kuni, the cook in the student cafeteria, that he was a great philosopher. Kuni played along with the joke, believing he deserved a university career. Students marched through the city demanding a lecturer's position for Jakob Kuni. One poster said "Was Pieck ist für die SED, ist Kuni

31

für Berlin WW" (What Pieck - the President of the DDR - is for the SED, Kuni is for West Berlin). Some of the demonstrations got a bit out of hand and my brother had to spend one night in a police cell.

In West Berlin I saw posters advertising the Investigations Committee of Freedom Lawyers who offered free legal advice to visitors from East Germany. As my mother had died early in 1949 I went to this group to get advice on inheritance questions. We three brothers were on a collision course with my father over my mother's modest inheritance. He wanted to invest in his shop but we thought it as a lost cause.

Once in the office of the Freedom Lawyers I did not hide my opposition to the Communist regime. I was asked to report on arrests and deportations, and to give names of Stasi spies. Thanks to my wide circle of acquaintances I could collect quite a lot of information fairly easily. I asked whether my activities in the LDP and the Association for German-Soviet Friendship were interpreted in the West as support for the East regime. I was told not to worry, that was not the case and that I should carry on. In any case, I had to be a member of the FDJ, the official youth organisation in East Germany, in order to attend a secondary school. As a secondary school student I was also obliged to take part in a multitude of political and social activities, such as demonstrations, harvest work in the countryside, attendance of political gatherings etc. Such political activity was a requirement for an eventual acceptance into university study in East Germany, which since 1949 had been called *Deutsche Demokratische Republik*.

The Telegram to Stalin

Erich Honecker, head of the FDJ, had a special idea for Stalin's birthday in December 1949: to send him a telegram signed by all pupils and students of the DDR. The cult idolatry around the person of Stalin reached an apogee in the text of the telegram where Stalin was hailed as the "genius of humanity". There were loud protesting voices throughout the school and there was the danger that virtually no one would sign the required text. We ex-members of the student council discussed among ourselves how we could best avoid conflict with the authorities. Some of the most disaffected students had already begun burning the text in the schoolyard.

We decided to come up with an alternative text that we could put to the students for their signature: "Most respected Generalissimus Stalin, We students of ….. promise to work hard for the good of society, to preserve peace, to cultivate friendships between nations… wish you good health…" As far as I can remember every student signed this text that we then gave to our school director to pass on to the authorities as far as Moscow. Our director as an old communist was a member of the SED. He taught history from a Soviet-Marxist point of view. He was understandably not particularly pleased with our initiative and tried, without success, to have us rescind our action.

Only a few days later, during a lesson, we heard loud voices out on the street. Three or four lorries from the local *VEB Bienertmühle* (Volkseigener Betrieb, a state-owned factory) had stopped in front of our school and workers on the open flat beds were shouting slogans aimed at our school through megaphones. They called for the closure of the school because students were reactionaries who did not deserve a high school education. Obviously this action by the workers was no spontaneous event but was rather organised by the authorities. We began to be anxious about the future of our school and permission to be able to take our final exams. In fact, 1950 was the last final exam at secondary school that still had a traditional curriculum including Latin and which would be fully recognised by the West.

On that same day I took the first train I could to Berlin. At that time the three Western Sectors were not yet segregated from the Eastern Sector. The infamous Berlin wall was erected much later. One could walk or travel from one Sector to another without interference. I went to the Freedom Lawyers and described our situation to them.

I was advised that we should avoid the closure of the school at all cost. The best solution would be to have one of the original members who started the initiative claim all responsibility and guilt. He would then probably be kicked out of the school. He could come to West Berlin where the Freedom Lawyers would organize a bursary for him to finish his schooling and then go on to university.

I was tempted to take on this role of scapegoat but I didn't want to leave my father - we had just lost my mother and my older brother had moved away to Berlin. So I went to Helmut Otto, a friend and co-initiator of our school action. He lived next door to us in the Bayreuther Street. I knew he planned to go to the West after his final exams. He was in fact willing to play the role of the scapegoat.

The sequence of events ran as predicted: assembly of all students in the auditorium, Helmut's admission of guilt, promise by the students to behave in a more "regime friendly" way. Thus we learned how to give lip service to save our skins. Helmut was expelled from school. He reported in to the Freedom Lawyers and received a year's bursary for secondary school and then a further grant to study politics at the *Freie Universität*.

Our classroom where we drafted our own text for the telegram to be sent to Stalin, according to the motto on the wall "Our country has to replace the lost material goods by intellectual wealth."

GESELLSCHAFTLICHE ARBEIT.

Ernst Jochen Erler.

Dresden, 28. Juni 1950
14. März 1951

Beteiligung an folgenden Arbeitseinsätzen:

Oktober 1945-Juli 1946: Sonntagseinsätze zwecks Zuschüttung von Wasser-
und Schützengräben in Dresden-Plauen und Räcknitz.

laufende Aufbauarbeiten an der zerstörten Oberschule Dresden-Süd.

26.5.48-14.7.48: In Hambinda in Thüringen Abbauarbeiten eines Rittergutes
und Aufbau von Neubauernhöfen (180 Arbeitsstunden).

11.6.-14.7.48: Großangelegte Thüringen-Borkenkäferaktion. Schulunterricht
fiel aus, da den ganzen Tag lang gearbeitet wurde.

Herbst 48: Aufbau und Vorrichtung der Versuchsanlagen im Chemie-Experi-
mentierraum der Schule.

Herbst 48-Sommer 49: Ziegelbergungsaktionen für unsere Neubauern.

16.1.49: Arbeitseinsatz "Hilfe für das Stahlwerk Döhlen".

26.3.50:   "Hilfe für das Stahlwerk Döhlen" gemeinsam mit der
Dresdner VVN.

Aktiver Einsatz und starke Mitarbeit an sämtlichen Arbeitseinsätzen,
die von der Schulklasse durchgeführt wurden, und an der Ausschmückung des
Klassenzimmers im Rahmen eines Wettbewerbes.

Tätigkeit in politischen Organisationen:

FDJ: Mitglied des Jugendkulturrings seit 1948 (Mitgl.Nr.2416).

Arbeit in der Wohngruppe Dresden Süd/Räcknitz. Funktionen:

Kulturfunktionär, Leiter des Zirkels zum Studium der Verfassung der DDR,
Mitarbeiter in der Laienspielgruppe. *Kulturfunktionär im Stadt-, Landes-
amt*

LDP: Mitglied seit 1948 (Mitgl.Nr.2354).

Gründung der LDP-Schülergruppe; Vorstandsmitglied des Jugend-Beirats
der Schule- und der Stadtgruppe Süd/Räcknitz. Funktion: Verbindungsmann
zur FDJ.   *Sommer 1950: Landesparteischule Rackebeul; Lehr-
gang für Student. Bewer-
ber.*

Mitarbeiter in der Hauptbetriebsgruppe-Schulen.
Teilnahme an den Jugend-Beirats-Tagungen.

DSF: Mitglied seit 1948 (Mitgl.Nr.1902).

Vorstandsmitglied der Gruppe des 8.Stadtbezirkes. Funktion: Verbindungsmann zur FDJ.

NF: Vorstandsmitglied der Gruppe des 8.Stadtbezirkes. *Literaturobmann
Kreisleiter des NF
Teilnahme an Kreisleiter-
Schulung.*

Sonstige gesellschaftliche Arbeit:

Teilnahme an sämtlichen Demonstrationen und Feiern.

Aktiver Einsatz bei der Unterschriftensammlung gegen die Atomwaffe.

Freie Deutsche Jugend
Kreisvorstand Dresden
Wohngruppe Süd-Räcknitz
Eigenschaftssatz 60,1.

K. Mond
(Gruppenleiter)

(Gruppenleiterin)   Freie Deutsche Jugend
Schulgruppe Dresden-Süd

Students were obliged to participate in officially organised activities. This is the certification by my school and the FDJ regarding my involvement. Such a list was a precondition for admission to university.

36

PARTICIPATION IN SOCIAL, POLITICAL AND COMMUNITY ACTIVITIES

Ernst Jochen Erler   Dresden 28 June 1950

Work activities

October 1945 - July 1946: filling in WWII trenches around Dresden on Sundays; reconstruction of our school in Dresden
26.5.48 - 14.7.48: in Haubinda, Thuringia, dismantling a manor and construction of houses for new farmers (180 workhours)
11.6. - 14.7.48: forestry work as part of a campaign against bark beetle
Fall 1948: installation of a chemistry laboratory in our school
Fall 1948 - Summer 1949: recuperation of bricks from city ruins for construction
16.1.49: work at the Steelworks in Döhlen
26.3.50: work at the Steelworks in Döhlen jointly with the Dresden VVN
Participation in all activities was undertaken by my class, including the decoration of our classroom in the context of a competition.

Political activities

FDJ: member of the Youth Cultural Association since 1948; in my local branch: responsible for cultural affairs, participant in a study group of the constitution, member of the amateur theatre group
LDP: member since 1948; cofounder of the LDP group at our school; board member of the local and school branch; participant in seminars
DSF: member since 1948; board member of the 9th district branch
NF: board member of the 9th district branch
Other activities: participation in demonstrations and celebrations; collection of signatures for petitions against atomic weapons

Translation

The Incriminating Leaflet

I finished high school and applied without success to universities in Leipzig and East Berlin. As a child of a former "capitalist", I was not admitted. I started work at the statistical office in Dresden.

One of my friends nicknamed Fupo wanted to be a *Volksrichter* (people's judge). I was appalled: such judges never dealt in justice but were purely representatives of the system. One of the Freedom Lawyers' fliers warned DDR citizens not to take up this profession because they would make themselves punishable after reunification - they would be held responsible for any violation of human rights according to international and West-German standards of justice.

In August 1950, I brought back one of these fliers from West Berlin and gave it to Fupo. I asked him under no circumstances to show it to anyone else, and to give it back to me. When I asked him for it a few days later, he said he'd burned it. I didn't believe him, but what could I do? Later I learned that he had shown the leaflet to our friend Günther Hastenrath who was our common friend and also a member of the LDP, one of the communist-controlled political parties in East Germany. Günther was also playing with the idea of becoming a *Volksrichter* judge. Years later my brother told me that after I was arrested, Günther fled to West Berlin and admitted to him in tears, that he had "sung". Günther had himself been arrested in Dresden as a member of an anti-government group (about which I had no idea). He was released though, when he promised to help the Stasi and denounced at least me to them.

Eberhard Fuchs, nicknamed Fupo, and Günther Hastenrath, friends from my Dresden neighbourhood and co-members of the LDP, told the Stasi about my connections with the West.

Under Surveillance by the Stasi

Four different incidents revealed I must have been under observation for about a year by the Stasi.

Firstly, a FDJ member whom I had met in East Berlin at one of the Youth Festivals visited me. I had already been suspicious of him. He asked me to type up a confirmation of an incident on my typewriter. It was obvious that the secret police wanted an example from my typewriter. He then asked me if I had any newspapers or other printed items from the West. He would love to read some Western material. He claimed to be a member of the *Zeugen Jehovas* (Jehova's Witnesses), a Christian sect not allowed in East Germany. I told him, and it was the truth, that I only had some old copies of the *Jugendtelegraph*, a newspaper from West Berlin. I gave him these old, yellowed issues from the years 1947-48, which at that time had been legal in East Germany.

Secondly, I had noticed that on two of my trips to Berlin one of the male passengers had tried to engage me in conversation and had shown interest in where I was going to get off. Both times I was able to get away by getting out abruptly at a different stop shortly before the terminus.

Thirdly, it was clear that our telephone was bugged. One could hear some suspicious clicks on the line. And in the last few days before my arrest I had noticed suspicious characters hanging around our street and watching the entrance to our house. So I often left the house by the back way over the rear courtyard and through the ruins of the adjacent property, to avoid being seen.

Fourthly, two friends warned me. Joachim Berthold, who was a LDP member of the Dresden city council, told me a few days before my arrest that my Stasi file was already quite large and I should reckon with being detained. I also ignored Günther Hastenrath's warning on the very day of my arrest when I met him - coincidentally? - on my way to the train station.

On the one hand I felt safe. I was a loner in my activities and had never revealed them to anybody else. The only thing that could compromise me was the Freedom Lawyers' flier. I did not consider myself to have broken the law of *Boykotthetze* (public anti-government propaganda) according to Article 6 of the German Democratic Republic's Constitution. I had only brought the poster to show it to my friend and had told him under no circumstances to pass it on to anyone else. Even though I did not believe Fupo when he said he had burned the flier, I had forbidden him spreading it further. If I had asked him to circulate this pamphlet, I could have committed *Boykotthetze*, propaganda against the DDR under Article 6 of the DDR Constitution. In my opinion, bringing a flier for personal information did not fulfill the criteria for *Boykotthetze*, which is an act in the public domain. At least so I thought in my naivety.

In addition, it did not surprise me that the Stasi had a file on me: I was from a "capitalist" family and had a brother who had moved to West Berlin.

On the other hand I did not trust Joachim Berthold or our common acquaintance Günther Hastenrath. Both were active in the LPD and it was no secret that in order to make a career, one had to conform to the system. I could not ignore the possibility that both had warned me in order to observe my reactions to such a warning, and to report it to the Stasi. In retrospect I admit that I behaved rather irresponsibly by not heeding their warnings and promptly fleeing to the West in good time.

I had to be very careful. At any moment I could be detained. When I prepared the last of my regular trips to Berlin, I hid a photo of a Stasi collaborator in the insole of my shoe. This man was known to travel often to West Berlin for shopping there. This photo could have been useful to the Western secret services because they could have tried to turn him into a *mole* within the Stasi. In the event of arrest and a successful total body search, this photo would have been highly incriminating for me.

Arrest and Interrogation by the Russians and Stasi

On 2 August 1951 it happened. As I was about to board the train to Berlin at the Dresden Main Train Station, I was arrested by two security officials in plain clothes without anybody noticing it. They took me inconspicuously to their car and drove to the police headquarters in the Schießgasse. First, my baggage was searched and I had a body search including my clothes. They found some rather unimportant papers and a list of lawyers that I had copied from the phone book. The Freedom Lawyers had asked me to obtain this information for them.

The interrogation was polite and correct. Early on it became clear to me that they knew about the Freedom Lawyers' flier. I admitted to having contact with that organisation. To appear believable I admitted without pressure from the investigators that I had supplied lists of members of the city and county councils and other openly accessible information to West Berlin.

41

But I was silent about all my other misdeeds, and there were plenty of them. For instance, I had taken photos of work camps in the Erzgebirge mountains where prisoners were forced to work for the Russian mining company Wismuth in the uranium mines. I had also regularly reported about arrests and had passed on the names of Stasi members. Among the latter were many *Hausobleute* (janitors) with whom one had to register travel coming and going and overnight visitors. All of them worked for the Stasi, whether they wanted it or not. The names of these Stasi collaborators, which had been reported to the various anti-communist organisations in West Berlin (League of Human Rights, Ostbüro of the SPD, Freedom Lawyers etc.), were finally made known by a RIAS broadcasting. I also didn't mention my role in the affair of the Stalin-birthday telegram at school.

The investigating officials were especially keen to find out if I was a member of an opposition group. I had a large number of friends and acquaintances, who often travelled to West Berlin. It was certainly possible that they were involved in illegal activities aside from black marketing. It was the truth when I stated that I did not know of any illegal political activities of my friends or acquaintances. Of course I knew about business friends of my parents who had illegally shipped machines to West Germany when the border was still open, and who were planning their flight to the West. Almost all of my friends and acquaintances were regular listeners to Western radio stations. But I did not mention any names, except Fupo's, to whom I had given the flyer. I needed to have him say that the flyer was for his eyes alone, for his personal information. I hoped to be released following his interrogation as my defense witness.

The interrogating security officials made it clear that my contacts with the Freedom Lawyers, especially having brought in the flier was punishable and this would result in many years of prison. They told me that instead of handing me over to the Stasi for interrogation and prosecution, they would prefer to recruit me to work for them. I could take the next train to Berlin and should continue my activities for the Freedom Lawyers and the League of Human Rights but maintain this in the interest of the DDR. In other words I should become a *mole* in the Western organisations. Nobody would know about my new orientation. Thanks to my many contacts in Dresden I would make a good conspiratorial collaborator for them.

I showed myself ready to cooperate but had in mind of course to escape to the West. Unfortunately it was not all that easy because the officials wanted something in exchange: I had to give them immediately the names of two people who had made themselves punishable by law in the DDR. I said I did not know any such people. Under no circumstances was I going to buy my freedom through betrayal. With that, the interrogation came to an end and I was locked in a cell where I went over and over in my head what could happen next: less correct interrogations, perhaps even torture or so-called truth serum injections. In any case, I opened up my insole and swallowed the photo. I did not trust the toilet in the cell because its contents could have perhaps been checked.

Later I found out that the officials who had arrested me were members of the so-called *Querapparat*, an organisation of formerly exiled Germans with Soviet citizenship who worked in liaison between the Soviet Secret Police (KGB) and the East German Secret Police, the Stasi. At my debriefing by the secret services of the Western powers after my escape to West Berlin I was told that the West had not been able to infiltrate the *Querapparat* by a mole while some of their agents had infiltrated the Stasi as moles.

Finally after hours of waiting, I was taken out of the cell and taken in a windowless prisoner transport van to a different building. The trip lasted about 15 minutes so I was still in the city precincts of Dresden. Later I found out that it was an ex-military prison in the Proschübel Strasse where Russian soldiers were now quartered and the Stasi conducted their interrogations.

Again I was left to wait many long hours in the cell. Late in the evening a new interrogation began. A single Russian officer conducted it: very correct, almost politely. He offered me cigarettes and gave me the impression that he had no doubts about the truth of my testimony.

After the investigation, that lasted till very late at night, I was brought to another cell: about 5 m long and 3 m wide with a high-barred window. Even if I could have reached the window it would have been impossible to get an object out of the cell: outside the bars there was a metal shield that impeded any communication. In the cell, the simple metal bed had been folded up against the wall; the tiny table and stool were bolted securely to both the floor and the wall. A covered pot stood in the corner of the cell and it stank of quicklime. The guards could look unnoticed into the cell by means of a spyhole in the door. At night I was allowed to pull down the bed along with a jute sack filled with straw and could sleep, lying on my back, my head toward the door, with my hands visible outside the wool blanket. Above the door there was a light that shone harshly on the bed all night. In the event that the guard would see me turned over in my sleep, he would immediately bang on the door.

Since sleep was permitted from 11 pm to 5 am and I had been brought to the cell well past midnight, that first night I had to make do with very few hours' sleep. I had also missed the evening meal due to the interrogation. Sleeping was not allowed during the day even when sitting on the stool. Breakfast consisted of four thin slices of bread coated with watery jam and a cup of *Kaffee Ersatz*, a substitute for coffee made from

44

chicory root. I was dead-tired and very hungry. Unfortunately this was soon established as my constant state of being. Interrogations were nearly every night at first and then only once in a while. They always started shortly before the distribution of dinner, which was four slices of bread with a thin layer of liver sausage and a cup of tea. So with every interrogation always at night, I missed dinner and was that much more pleased to have lunch, which was a bowl of watery stew.

The condition of permanent hunger was well known to me from the last weeks of the war and the early post-war years. But other things gnawed away at me: continuously being enclosed in a cell in complete isolation led to brooding and worrying about how much the Russians and the Stasi might know about me. This was wearing me down because it was known that they had their own agents in the Western anti-communist organisations. I feared the Stasi would search our apartment and find some incriminating items that my father may have stashed. There was also the danger that my father would be indicted for complicity in my activity.

The Russian officer only carried out three nighttime interrogation sessions. Then I suddenly stood in front of a new face: a German who spoke in a heavy Saxon dialect and who took me through 24 more interrogations. His behaviour was in stark contrast to the business-like way the Russian had conducted the interrogation. Often he became furious, screamed at me, hit me and kicked me with his boots in my buttocks. Twice I fell unconscious from his treatment, after my head had become suddenly hot and the world had turned black before my eyes. I awoke in my cell and had difficulty remembering the interrogation I had just been through.

At one point of deep desperation I tried to commit suicide in my cell. The only device that I had to cut open a vein was my glass eye. I managed to break the glass eye but the attempt was in vain: the edges were not sharp enough to cut even my skin. In my emotional upset I had overlooked the fact that the glass eye had the properties of high quality porcelain and not glass. The next morning the guard accepted my explanation that the glass eye had fallen and broken when I washed my face and rinsed the eye cavity.

During one of the sessions my interrogator stated that my older brother had been arrested during a trip to Dresden and had admitted to his collaboration with me. I immediately could see this was a bluff. In the first place, I never told my brother about my activities. Secondly, I knew that my brother would never again travel into the DDR for safety reasons. It turned out during the course of the interrogation, that the Stasi believed it was my brother who had made contact with the office of the Freedom Lawyers. Someone of the Eastern secret police had seen me wearing my brother's motorbike gear and riding his motorbike on one of my visits to the office of the Freedom Lawyers.

After several sessions the interrogating officer gave me some paper and a pencil to write down the name of every person in my circle of friends and acquaintances along with their Western contacts and their political stances. A few days later I was supposed to present my Western contacts in chronological order. Some time later I had to describe the venues of meetings I had in West Berlin. They also demanded a sketch of the office of the Freedom Lawyers. After a break of a few weeks, I had to describe everything again including people and places in chronological order.

This way the Stasi could compare my oral statements during the interrogation with what I wrote down. They found no discrepancies and so I escaped the injection of the so-called "truth serums" and the especially feared *U-Boot*, the former

46

Gestapo underground torture cells used by the Russians in East Berlin and later by the Stasi to make political prisoners speak. As I later learned from other prisoners, there were narrow cells where it was impossible to move, where the prisoners had water dripping on their heads for hours or even days. In another Russian prison it was said there were narrow round spaces like baking ovens where the prisoner was shoved in like bread dough and heated up. It is doubtful though that in 1950 when the Stasi was created as the follow-on organisation from the K5 unit of the police, such medieval methods were used. Confessions could be obtained with modern drugs.

My arrest would lead without problem to my release, so I thought. The trips to Berlin were to visit my brother who was studying at the *Freie Universität* there. Naturally I did not mention my black marketing activities. My contacts with the Committee of the Freedom Lawyers I attributed to their free advice offered to DDR citizens. It was even true that I had sought advice with regard to my mother's inheritance. So nothing illegal! Admittedly from my first contact with the Freedom Lawyers further visits had developed. Without particular effort I could provide this organisation with lists of addresses of local politicians, lawyers and so forth. In my opinion, this was not against the law. None of the lists contained any secret information because all the names and addresses were openly available to anyone; they were in the public domain.

Aside from reimbursement of my train travel costs I had received no payments. I always refused to take fliers to Dresden for distribution or to do any conspiratorial activity. Personally I consider spying immoral, and did not believe in the effectiveness of fliers being distributed to the public. During Hitler's time they did not show any result.

All along I had kept my own safety in mind: I did not want to fall foul of the law. I still had not given up hope of studying in the

East despite coming from a "capitalist" family. I wanted to stay in Dresden with my family, my friends and relations, and have available our weekend house in the Erzgebirge mountains.

My contact at the Freedom Lawyers was Dr Hamann, at least that was what I understood his name to be. He had introduced me to a refugee lawyer, Otto Schneider, in the German League for Human Rights. They both reassured me that I would be offered a scholarship to study if I came to the West, just as had happened for my friend Helmut Otto, who, after finishing high school in West Berlin, was then studying political science at the *Freie Universität*. I played this card toward my defense because it gave a believable reason for my continuing contact with the Freedom Lawyers.

Further to my defense, I emphasised that I had not brought the flier for the purpose of *Boykotthetze* but to give personal information to my friend Fupo. I asked the Stasi interrogator to bring in Fupo so that I could face him and prove I had asked him to give the flier back to me without showing anybody else. This request was denied.

The nighttime interrogations became rarer. I had nothing more to add. The constant repetition of my "story" pushed all memory of the truth aside till I believed completely in the half-truths I had concocted. If I had been given a "truth serum" at that point they probably would have pulled only these half-truths out of my subconscious!

During the course of the many weeks of my arrest, an almost friendly relationship had grown between a prison guard and me. He told me that he had been obliged as a party member to take up police work and was a prison guard against his will. Occasionally he gave me leftover food from older prisoners. I was even allowed to leave the cell to clean the guards' toilet and the corridors.

He admitted to watching a very pretty young woman through the spyhole. He allowed me to have a look as well. Later, in the Bautzen prison, I found out about her history from her partner and future husband Uwe Peterson. Even later in Heidelberg where I was a student I met Gisela myself. She had belonged to a student protest group that distributed and posted fliers.

This intermezzo from the monotonous life in my cell lasted only a few days. My interrogating officer saw me cleaning floors and gave the order not to allow me outside my cell anymore.

Police Prison and the Trial

After 16 weeks detention in the Proschübel Strasse prison I was brought to the official investigations prison in the Dresden Police headquarters in the Schießgasse. The cell was bigger there, the food better and I was allowed 30 minutes a day of fresh air. Although I was still in solitary confinement the policing did not seem as strict. I learned how to communicate with other prisoners in adjacent cells, by means of tapping signals, one tap for the letter A, two for B and so forth. As soon as the syllable or word had been understood a response signal was given. In this way we exchanged news - we had neither newspapers nor radio. The only news came from criminals freshly incarcerated. From rumours we found out that there may be an amnesty on the occasion of Stalin's birthday on 20 December. Since my trial in the county court was set for the 22 December, could I hope for release? In the end the guards confirmed there was to be an amnesty but not for economic or political prisoners.

The prisoners called out this news from cell to cell and the criminals were in high spirits. We political prisoners were depressed. I yelled out from my cell that Stalin was a mass murderer who had the blood of millions of Russians and Poles on his hands. A guard must have heard me because I was taken down to the bunker, an underground cell for three days. It was dark, cold and stuffy. The hard wooden bed had no blanket. I was given only water and dry bread.

After my transfer from the secret Stasi prison to the official police prison my father was informed about my arrest and the forthcoming court trial. For more than four months he had been without knowledge of my fate. Now he was allowed to visit me in the Schießgasse prison. Although he knew nothing about my contacts with the Freedom Lawyers and the League for Human Rights he had presumed I had been arrested. He hired a lawyer he knew, Dr Crusius, to take up my defense.

I did not trust the lawyer. Was it possible he also worked for the Stasi? Moreover I suspected that there were bugs, listening devices, built into the walls of the prison visiting room. A week later a new person appeared, a rather unpleasant individual. He looked to me like a Stasi spy. He presented himself as my counsel for the defense appointed by the court. He told me that Dr Crusius had given up my case. Later I found out that Dr Crusius was a collaborator with the Freedom Lawyers and had gone to West Berlin with my file.

My new defense lawyer made sure that I had the opportunity to get a new prosthetic eye. The glass blower, who was a good friend of our family - my father also had a glass eye - told my father about my appointment despite being forbidden to do so. When I was brought by three policemen in plainclothes to the eye clinic, my father could catch a glimpse of me from the distance. Due to my shortsightedness I did not see him waving at me, because my glasses had been taken away since my incarceration.

The trial date was made public. It was to be held at the county courthouse at the Münchner Platz in Dresden. By means of my defense lawyer I had asked my father not to come to the trial. I wanted to spare him the sad exhibition and was also afraid that he might give vent to his displeasure there.

I was surprised to see Eberhard Mehle, one of my best friends, amongst the public at the trial. As the son of an entrepreneur in whose family business he worked, he had always taken a critical stance vis-à-vis the system. It took quite a measure of courage to show up at my trial. Eberhard even behaved provocatively as he noisily pushed his chair back, stood up and made a show of leaving the courtroom. This was during the litany delivered by the state prosecutor in which I was described as a lackey of American imperialism. I was afraid for Eberhard. I found out later, though, that nothing untoward happened to him on account of his action.

For my defense I stuck to my old story: I had begun the contact with the West because of the no-cost legal advice I could get; I had only given over information that could be obtained anyway from publicly accessible media like telephone books and daily newspapers, and I

My friend Eberhard Mehle was the only person among my friends who attended my trial. My other friends had reason to fear being suspected as my sympathisers. Here, he is overdressed for a party.

had brought only one single flyer that I had given a friend with the promise, that he show it to no one else. I requested again and again without success, that my friend Fupo be allowed to speak in my defense. I showed regret for my actions and asked for lenience.

The judgment: six years in prison, loss of property and ten years obligatory civil restrictions, i.e. loss of civil rights, etc. "Better than Siberia," I said to myself. If they had known about my reports on the Wismuth labour camps, I would have been brought in front of a Russian tribunal and sent to Siberia.

Abschrift

I-2 103/51

U r t e i l

I m   N a m e n   d e s   V o l k e s !

In der Strafsache

gegen

den am 29.3.1932 in Dresden geborenen Lagerbuchhalter

Ernst Jochen E r l e r

wohnhaft in Dresden A 24, Bayreuther Strasse 32,
'.Zt. in Untersuchungshaft in der VP-Haftanstalt Dresden,
Schiessgasse

wegen Verbrechen nach Artikel 6 der Verfassung der DDR,
in Verbindung mit Kontrollratsdirektive 38, Abschnitt II,
Artikel III A III

hat die Strafkammer I-2 des Landgerichts Dresden in der
Sitzung vom 2o. Dezember 1951, an der teilgenommen haben:

Oberrichterin L ö w e
als Vorsitzende,
Landrichter S e i d l e r
als beisitzender Richter,

staatsanwaltschaft
a
_

Bernhard Jahn, Angestellter,
Otto Müller, Angestellter,
Johannes Somiesky, Versicherungsvertreter,
sämtlich in Dresden
als Schöffen,

las Urteil
: Angeklagte
12.51
.on eingelegt.

Staatsanwalt Stutzriemer
als Vertreter des Oberstaatsan-
waltes,

Protokollantin Schubert
als Schriftführerin,

für   R e c h t   erkannt:

Der Angeklagte Jochen   E r l e r   wird wegen Ver-
brechens nach Art. 6 d.Verf.d.DDR in Verbindung mit
KRDir. 38, Abschn. II, Art. III A III zu

6   -sechs- Jahren Zuchthaus

kostenpflichtig verurteilt.
Die obligatorischen Sühnemassnahmen der Dir.38,Art.IX,
Ziff. 2-9 werden angeordnet.
Die seit dem 2.8.1951 erlittene U.-Haft wird auf die
erkannte Strafe voll angerechnet.

The sentence to six years penitentiary, confiscation of the inheritance from my
mother, and other penal measures.

54

JUDGEMENT IN THE NAME OF THE PEOPLE

in the criminal proceedings against

the storebookkeeper, born on 29.3.1932 in Dresden,

Ernst Jochen E r l e r

residing in Dresden A 24, Bayreuther Strasse 32, at present in custody with the Police Prison Dresden, Schiessgasse,

on account of crime according to Article 6 of the DDR Constitution, in connection with Allied Control Council Directive 38, Section II, Article III A III,

the Division for Criminal Matters I-2 of the Dresden District Court in its session on 20 December 1951 in which participated:

Senior Judge Löwe as chairperson,
Judge Seidler as assisting judge

Bernhard Jahn, employee,
Otto Müller, employee,
Johannes Somiesky, insurance agent,
as jurors in Dresden

Stateprosecution:
State Prosecutor Stutzriemer as representative of the Senior State Prosecutor,
clerk Schubert as secretary.

The following verdict was rightfully recognised:

The accused Jochen E r l e r , because of a crime according to Art.6 d.Verf.d.DDR in connection with KRDir. 38, Sec. II, Art. III A III, is sentenced to
6 - six - years penitentiary
with liability to pay the costs.
The atonement measures of Dir. 38, Art. IX, Para. 2-9 are applied.
The period of custody since 2.8.1951 will fully count towards the imposed penalty.

Translation

First Penal Institution: Bautzen II

I spent the following weeks in the Schießgasse, Dresden's famous police prison. After the sentence had become final, I was put into a communal cell with other inmates. It was an amusing community. One of the inmates was an excellent conversationalist, a good-looking marriage swindler who had relieved lonely widows of their life savings. He had also excelled as a body-stripper of graves, amongst them the tomb of Albrecht Graf von Roon, Minister of War under Bismarck. He also had sold non-existent goods to trusting and gullible country vicars.

Our cell was within knocking and calling distance of the women's cells that were above ours. Our respective sexual needs were the dominant themes of our communication and we had a lot of fun albeit at a distance with the rather frivolous girls upstairs. Occasionally a secret message managed to reach us, let down on a string from window to window. Apparently the girls had paper and pencil - things which none of us had in possession.

Unfortunately my stay with this merry group lasted only a short while. One day, a black Maria police van took me to Bautzen II, an old prison building in the middle of the town of Bautzen. Most cells were over-crowded. Originally conceived for only one inmate, they now had two or three inmates. However, I was put in solitary confinement for quite a few weeks. I was disappointed, especially as I had enjoyed the companionship of fellow prisoners after having been sixteen weeks in my brooding.

Like all prisoners I was not allowed a radio, newspapers or writing materials. Only books by classic and modern pro-Communist writers, mostly editions from the East German Aufbau Verlag, including translations into German of the whole Russian literature and books on Marxism/Leninism were available. Textbooks for self-learning the Russian language were forbidden. We were supposed to sink into stupidity. Knocking on the walls was still the most important means of contact with fellow prisoners - but if we were caught doing it, it was off to the bunker. Once in a while we managed to whisper news to each other in the prison's courtyard: our names, how many years we were condemned to, the reason for our arrest, etc.

The Stasi Will Not Leave Me Alone

The monotonous existence of my solitary confinement was relieved by a newly arrived inmate by the name of Niemeyer. I later learned that he was a Stasi officer who had in some way made himself punishable by law and had to spend some weeks in prison, this not without a job. I underwent a new series of investigative sessions. I repeated my story, which by then I believed myself. Niemeyer managed to clarify a discrepancy in my story that I had not known existed. My contact at the Freedom Lawyers was not as I thought a Dr Hamann but rather a certain Dr Hermann. When first introduced to him, I had misunderstood his name, and at later meetings had always asked for Dr "Hamann". Under the threat of being punished otherwise, Niemeyer told me that I should keep silent about his function as a member of the Stasi as he had other inmates to sound out. However, the guards knew about his double role, and it was spread to the prisoners probably in the form of a warning. The guards themselves were afraid of the Stasi, and some of them had a kind of sympathy for the political prisoners.

After Niemeyer had left, I was transferred to a cell with two other inmates. Everyone knew that I had spent several weeks with Niemeyer in my cell and that Niemeyer was a spy. Still, not to jeopardize my situation I did not tell anyone that I had undergone a grilling from Niemeyer, that I was the victim of an intense interrogation by him. My denial that I would know about Niemeyer's background did not make my early years in Bautzen easy. None of my fellow inmates trusted me. I was suspected of also being a Stasi spy. This was an especially difficult time for me.

The new cell was built for single occupancy but was now overcrowded by us three men. However, I had some companionship even though elbowroom was severely restricted. In our cell we had to strip goose feathers that were then made into duvets. The stripping was exacting and boring work. The feathers had not yet been cleaned so they stank horribly. We had to move slowly and carefully about the cell, so as not to create any air movement that could lift the feathers into the air, causing us breathing difficulties.

One day, we were happy to be given boxes of screws, nuts, washers, bolts and other metal pieces that we had to sort out for purposes of re-use in the future. While it was still tedious work at least it was more hygienic and we could breathe normally.

Fellow Inmates

I could group the inmates with whom I shared my prison time into several categories. In the first category there were the true criminals who were in the minority. I got to know some very interesting members of this group. I had a good relationship with them since it was irrelevant to them whether or not I was a Stasi collaborator. In addition, the criminal types tended to have more backbone than the political prisoners. They had a code of honour and did not let themselves be duped by guards through cigarettes or other favours into making revelations about other prisoners. Unfortunately, some political prisoners were susceptible to being bribed into becoming denunciators.

Anyone who had wreaked damage on a bank, a church or an insurance company was a "gentleman". Practically all cheats including marriage swindlers and grave strippers belonged to this category. They looked down on small-time thieves with disdain, regarding them as the scum of life, for instance, vagabonds who stole laundry from the lines or who stole rabbits from private owners. Stealing bicycles was also seen as asocial. Bank robbers and counterfeiters of money were highly regarded. I never got to know any of these in Bautzen. Most of my fellow inmates were political prisoners, from Jesuits to Jehovah's Witnesses, from political satirists to those who had posted a political flier.

Then there was a large number of *Wirtschaftsverbrecher*, economic criminals. These were black market dealers, or workers and service personnel in the state-owned VEB factories, who had stolen "the peoples'" goods. Manufacturers also belonged to this group, who had tried to move their enterprises to the West, and business people who tried to dispose of their hoarded goods against hard currency in the West. Before the erection of a well-guarded fence between East and West Germany, and the creation of the two separate German states, there was a lively exchange in both directions of smuggling across borders. It was only later that the increasing stream of refugees out of the East lead to the virtually hermetic closure of the border between East and West Germany.

The majority, however, were true political prisoners. Most like me, had been condemned according to Article 6 of the DDR Constitution for the so-called *Boykotthetze* (hateful propaganda against the State), either because of a political joke, the spreading of news that was not in the interests of the regime, or communal listening to Western radio stations. Later on, when fleeing from the DDR became illegal, there were also prisoners who had tried or helped in escapes.

Only a very few inmates had actually been actively engaged against the regime: either distributing and sticking up posters and leaflets or delivering information for one of the many subversive organisations that had been established in West Berlin. Even Jehovah's Witnesses were considered an arm of Western imperialism and were condemned to many years of hard labour if they were caught distributing their writings and brochures.

In all my years of imprisonment I never met a real spy, who had worked for the American, British or French secret services. These professional agents were in other prisons and were often used for exchange deals between the East and the West.

A really amusing political inmate was the young woman with whom we male prisoners had already had contact through secret notes in the Dresden police prison. She had been a prostitute in Görlitz and had inadvertently taken a client's work permit when she had stolen his wallet. Unfortunately the client was a policeman in civil clothes. The crime became a political infringement against Article 6 of the DDR Constitution, which led to a political trial that ended in two years condemnation due to *Boykotthetze*.

I also met another category of prisoner when I was moved to the Gulag-like prison, the Yellow Misery. This category were people who had been condemned to up to four times 25 years internment by Russian courts before the founding of the DDR. These prisoners were people who had carried on fighting after the armistice (8 May 1945), who were former officials of the Hitler regime or were citizens in whose possession weapons had been found. The old hands of the prison inmates told us that as many as 16,000 prisoners had not survived the post-war hunger years from 1945 to 1949, mainly due to tuberculosis and undernourishment. They lay under a blanket of quicklime in deep covered trenches on the so-called Rabbit Hill. Those who had survived were the first to be released from Soviet camps and later from DDR labour camps and prisons following the advent of Perestroika, the end of Stalin's terror thanks to Khrushchev.

Bautzen I - The Yellow Misery

After having spent about four months in the Bautzen II building, a former police prison and then a Stasi prison in the middle of Bautzen, I was moved in a group transporter to the infamous Bautzen I prison on the edge of town, called the *Yellow Misery* for its yellow walls and the brutality of its guards. What a contrast! Here more than a thousand inmates were kept in military-like order and discipline in extremely close quarters.

My narrow sleeping space was in a dormitory that had bunk beds for 220 men. This reminded me of pictures I had seen of concentration camps but fortunately people here were only occasionally undernourished and did not have the skin and bones of victims of Hitler's Third Reich. Between the long rows of bunks there were narrow passageways that during the day were always congested with people who were congregating to talk. Only 30 minutes a day were allocated for *Rundgang*, a walk in the courtyard one after another where we were not allowed to speak or exchange signs. We spent most of our time on our bunks, reading or playing chess. My fellow inmate Walter Kempowski described circumstances in minute detail in his book *Im Block*, as did Wolfgang Hardegen in *Imprisoned in Bautzen*.

There was a kind of self-governance among the inmates. The *Saalältester* (hall leader) - called *Kapo* in the concentration camps - was responsible for quiet, orderliness and cleanliness. He was appointed by the prison governor. His assistants were the *Kalfaktoren* who retrieved the food from the central kitchen and distributed it among us. They also looked after our soap, bed linen and prison garb. The hall leaders suggested the names of potential *Kalfaktoren* to the administration. In general the hall leaders and their assistants were suspected of denouncing inmates in order to make themselves popular with the administration and so to get released earlier. I was not sure whether my hall leader, called "Paddlehand" because of his crippled hand, was one of those types. In any event I kept a careful distance from this man who treated us severely, like a sergeant his field recruits.

Prison activities run exclusively by inmates included the kitchen, a hospital, a dentist, a church choir and a youth choir. The kitchen and hospital were the favoured work places because there was better food there. The kitchen was especially popular because they also cooked for the women's sector of the prison and there was contact with the female *Kalfaktors*. Our *Kalfaktors* were envied for this contact they had with women. Since I had neither medical nor gastronomical talents, but did have some knowledge of music and a good singing voice I signed up for the youth choir. I was not interested in the church choir and anyway I heard them when I went to the prison chapel once a month.

The youth choir presented a cultural program and had a lot of practice meetings, which provided a regular change from the monotonous daily prison routine. Moreover we could learn harmonic theory from the choir director who was a music teacher from Bremen. Our repertory, a *cappella* only, consisted of medieval love songs, folk songs and opera choruses. I was a first bass. To this day, I remember many lovely melodies that I learned while in prison.

Our main preoccupation as prisoners was how to survive this time of huge psychological stress and physical weakness. We organised physical fitness sessions because the daily *Rundgang* session in the courtyard was not enough exercise. We slept with an open window even in the coldest weather, in order to get some fresh air into the stuffy, crowded cell or hall.

In my previous Bautzen II cell, I had been assigned to the upper bunk bed right under a window. In the morning, after a cold night, I sometimes found frost at the end of my blanket from my breathing. The straw-filled jute sack that served as a mattress and the single wool blanket did not keep me warm enough so I usually slept in my day clothes. Now in Bautzen I, my bed was in the middle of a huge assembly of double-level beds. There was a saying "besser warmer Mief als kalter Ozone" (better warm stink than cold ozone).

We tried to keep *mens sana* alongside our effort of a *corpus sanum* and so make use of our brains when we could. It was not allowed to take any instruction books out of the library. So we studied chess theory and played chess nearly every day. There were some inmates who developed into real stars, playing blind and simultaneously, and winning most of their games.

Another mental occupation was group classes in foreign languages, without a textbook of course and without pen and paper. Instead we used the occasional piece of slate tile that had fallen off the roof, with a small piece of aluminium wire for the writing. The former chief editor at the *Reclam* publishing company could have taught us nearly all the major languages of the world. I learned French, which I had not been able to do in high school due to the predominance of Russian (also Latin and English). I could have also learned Chinese or Arabic in Bautzen I. It was thanks to these French classes that within a year of my release I got a bursary from the *DAAD* (German Academic Exchange Service) to study in Lausanne, Switzerland.

Work Assignment

Aside from the service units in the prison, such as kitchen, hospital, laundry, library etc. that were all run by inmates, there were also proper industries within the prison walls that kept the majority of prisoners occupied. Apart from an engineering office there were several industrial units within the Bautzen I compound. These production zones were extensions of state-owned companies, VEBs.

By comparison, work outside the prison walls - the building of a landing strip for airplanes offered a unique opportunity to have some healthy work in the fresh air. I signed up for work on the landing strip. The 30-minute promenade with a few exercises in the prison courtyard was not enough for me. Alas, I was considered unfit for physical work because of my crippled right hand. Instead, the prison administration made me the wage clerk for the state-owned *Sächsische Kleiderwerke*, a dress making business, with some 200 prisoners working there in two shifts. I had learned bookkeeping at extension school during my high school time. My job was enviable: I had my own office, an electric calculator and more importantly paper and pencils! I received a normal salary, with the imprisonment costs taken out. The rest of the money went to a *Sperrkonto*, a blocked savings account. On and off we were allowed to use a small amount (8% of our salary) to buy food, personal hygiene articles and cigarettes. But only occasionally: it all depended on the economic situation in the DDR! Anyway, no inmates ever got a penny of that blocked money when released, either from the DDR officials or the Federal Republic of Germany after reunification. Even I who had looked after the income of 220 prison workers was denied my request for repayment after the reunification of Germany on the basis of "insufficient evidence". Statements made by fellow inmates were not accepted as proof. Conceivably this was an infringement of our constitutional rights of equality (equal treatment for the victims of Fascism and the victims of Stalinism)! Well, never mind. I got tired of strife with bureaucracies.

I did quite well as a bookkeeper in my office. A few guards brought me cake and cigarettes. One went so far as to confide in me that he was about to escape to the West. He told me that he had been a driver for my father before the war. I asked him questions about the store, the delivery vans and my father's habits (as an early riser he always started the fire in the furnace). The guard answered correctly in all cases. He asked me, if I would like to send any information to the West. I declined his offer. The Western organisations were infiltrated by the Stasi and I did not want to take any risks at all. Anyway, what could I have told him? One day this guard simply disappeared.

The days surrounding the 17 June 1953, the People's Uprising in the DDR against the regime, were exciting for us. Outside the prison walls, workers from a nearby VEB shouted in unison demands for our release. The guards ordered the shaving off of our hair so that in case we escaped or were freed we would easily be recognised for what we were and rounded up again. In nearby Görlitz the workers at the train car factory had stormed the women's prison and had freed the inmates there. Thundering motors and rattling chains soon put an end to our hopes: tanks had surrounded the Yellow Misery.

Most of the guards got scared though. They suddenly became friendly towards us and asked suggestively whether they had not always treated us well. This apparent change in tone and atmosphere led to a tragic misunderstanding by two of my friends and comrades: Ernst Schnabel, a member of the *Herrnhuter Gemeinschaft* (a movement within the Protestant Church) and researcher on Schopenhauer, and Horst Köhler, an actor. As the work on the landing strip started up again after the uprising had been suppressed, the two men trusted the new climate amongst the guards and tried to flee. None of the guards shot into the air and both friends were brought back to the Yellow Misery as corpses.

Illness

Every two years each inmate was given an x-ray because of a high incidence of tuberculosis in the prison. My x-rays showed a shadow in the lungs but my body had enough immunity to stifle the tuberculosis. Whoever had a clear open case of TB was isolated in the TB-station where chances of survival were not promising. At some point, though, my liver began to have problems. Over the many years, we did not receive any meat with the exception of maggots in the pea and lentil soups, and mostly ate sauerkraut, cabbage, beets and potatoes for lunch, the only warm meal. For breakfast and dinner we received the same meager offering as in the prisons before: slices of bread. This diet led to jaundice. I was put on a special diet and got more flour-based dishes than before. In addition I had permanent gastritis, like so many of my fellow prisoners.

One day I had tremendous abdominal pains. Fortunately they were diagnosed in good time as appendicitis and I was taken to the prisoners' hospital where the surgeon Dr Behne, like us a political prisoner, was working. He was a former student of the famous Professor Sauerbruch of Berlin's Charité. After his release and escape to West Germany in 1956, Dr Behne received the highest decoration of Germany, the *Bundesverdienstkreuz*, Germany's Pour le Mérite.

My stay in the prisoner's hospital was a gift from heaven. While I was under anaesthetic the inmates treating me could ask me about my past activities. As I have explained, I had the reputation of not being a trustworthy prisoner. For that reason I was avoided by many co-inmates and was left without any sense of comradeship with those sharing my fate. Thanks to the questioning while I was under anaesthetic my position became immediately different. Quickly word went around that I was clean and not a spy. Suddenly all my co-inmates were friendly to me, and I could have joined a resistance group.

After my release, I learned that there was a unit involved in dismantling defective appliances in order to get parts for recycled use. Several clever guys built a radio with such parts and it was hidden under the floor of their workhouse barracks. For years contact with the outside was kept going.

One of my comrades tried to recruit me to the Jesuits. He assured me that being a believer was of secondary importance. Such a career would have provided me with an education without financial worries and would have guaranteed an interesting political existence. But I wanted to remain an honest freethinker, to retain my freedom of thought.

Transfer to My Third Penitentiary: Waldheim

My rather agreeable - given the circumstances - life as a payroll bookkeeper came to an unexpected end in 1955. I was transferred to the Zuchthaus Waldheim (a penitentiary) with a higher percentage of ordinary criminals than I had encountered in Bautzen. We prisoners never understood the rationale of the prison service with regard to which facility one was assigned. There were no evident criteria for why some had to serve their sentence in Bautzen and others in Waldheim. In any event Waldheim did not have the bad reputation that Bautzen had, where almost 20,000 former prisoners lay buried under a thick layer of quicklime.

Waldheim prison was an old building, unlike the huge Bautzen I complex. Prisoners spent their free time in halls that held 120 people. Cells were for sleeping and had been designed (at the time when Karl May, the famous writer of adventure books was imprisoned there) for only one prisoner. When I was there, three people were crowded into a cell. As in all prison facilities in the DDR, most of the inmates worked in production sites that had been set up by VEBs inside the prison walls. The inmates in my hall worked in a *Silberschleiferei*, a unit for polishing silverware. As this work is considered dangerous to health, the workers received milk.

Due to my crippled hand I was not able to work there. Thus I spent my time reading books and playing chess with comrades who were not on shift. I offered a helping hand to Willi Franke, our *Saalältester* - a kind of supervisor in charge of about 120 prisoners in a given hall. He was jailed for so-called economic crimes and was a robust sort of man who must have been a tough sergeant in the army. Before distributing the food he would fish out the few bits of ham fat from the pot for himself. What made him particularly unpopular with his fellow prisoners, was his willingness to denounce fellow prisoners and bow to the guards.

As a Saalältester

One day the prison director, Kommissar Wiese, called me to his office. "Erler, you will henceforth take over as *Saalältester* from Franke." The order sent a shock through me because I in no way wanted to be a hated *Kapo* who was a kind of kowtow to the prison guards. I tried to change the director's mind by explaining what a softie I was, especially with the hardened criminals who needed a toughness bordering on brutality in order to gain respect and authority over them. Wiese replied that he knew about my popularity in the hall and that I would have free rein in terms of my methods for keeping the men in order. He told me to sleep on the proposal and come back to him about it the next day.

When I returned to the hall Willi Franke had already been removed - it looked like a *fait accompli* to me. Nevertheless I did not want to take up the post without obtaining acceptance and support of the men in the hall. After the food had been distributed, I told them about Wiese's decision and explained that I would only accept the position if the inmates trusted me and would support me in the job. Failing this, I would rather spend time in the bunker than put my future on the line after being released from prison. It was my opinion that the majority of the Saalältesten made themselves punishable by law for assisting in crimes against human rights.

Due to the unpopularity of Willi I reckoned a majority of voices would be in my favour. To my pleasant surprise the vote was unanimous in my favour. I could rest comfortably. The next morning I reported the vote to Wiese. He was furious. "We are not a democracy here!" he said in his unmistakable Saxon dialect. He could send me to the bunker for that. I responded that I would rather be put in the bunker than become a denunciator. Wiese acted as though he were astounded that I thought he was interested in denunciations. He said he got enough in- formation from the wardens, prison guards and also from prisoners of course. It was inmates who initiated denunciations, he said. For his part, he wanted peace and quiet and expected me to ensure cleanliness and order in the hall. This attitude was very plausible because as an old Communist, Wiese had spent years in Nazi imprisonment. He must have also hated denunciators. There is a saying in German: "Man liebt den Verrat, aber nicht den Verräter" (Betrayal is welcome, but not the betrayer).

The eighteen months that I was Saalältester in charge of one of the halls in Waldheim were peaceful. There were only two events which I haven't forgotten. The first was when a fellow inmate had stolen sugar from another inmate's cupboard. I told everyone in the hall about the theft and ordered the thief to return the stolen sugar at the earliest opportunity. Then I left the hall so that I would not be witness to what was carried out as the inmates' own form of justice. When I came back into the hall ten minutes later it was quiet. The thief sat in a corner with a black eye; he had suffered quite a thrashing. I ignored him and the incident. At a later meeting, I learned from Kommissar Wiese that the inmates felt that I had handled the situation correctly, and he agreed. Officially, he added laughing, he would of course have to criticize my action.

The other incident took place shortly before Christmas 1955. Because the DDR was once again short of many food items like butter, sugar etc., inmates were not permitted to buy any food. We also were not allowed to get our monthly gift parcel from home. The latter prohibition hit us harder than the first because we all received rare foodstuff from home. We all ate a regular dose of garlic, one clove a day, in order to protect ourselves from infections. Our supply was now blocked. However, one day we were suddenly given a list of goods that we could purchase with the money in our prison savings accounts in order to send packages home! Since the list also included rare food items, we interpreted this offer as pure propaganda. While we dined on a watery steamed cabbage soup we were supposed to send home butter and bacon so that they got the impression that we got these foods in prison! Moreover we had never had the opportunity to send presents home before. Together with other like-minded inmates, I organised a boycott. All the men in my hall joined in - both the political and criminal prisoners. Only one of the inmates, whose marriage was on the rocks, sent a child's toy, but no food. We had all encouraged him not to join the boycott.

One day, as I was sitting at the end of the hall reading a book I saw a high-ranking police officer come through the door at the other side of the hall. I was supposed to call "Achtung!" (attention) and rush over to the officer with this information: "Prisoner Erler with 20 prisoners present, all on free time." However, I opted for passive resistance and pretended I had not noticed the officer. One of the other inmates called "Attention!" I jumped up and gave my report. The officer yelled at me for overlooking him. Then he took me out into the stairwell. It was a circular flight of stairs, like in a medieval tower. He asked me who had organised the boycott in our hall. No other hall had engaged in such an action.

I told him it had just spontaneously sprung up. There was general opposition to the offer of sending parcels home at a time when we were not allowed to buy food items or receive parcels. The inmates worked hard in the silver polishing unit, fulfilled the quota requirements and got their money but still - in spite of their hunger - could not buy food for themselves. I told the officer that this had embittered the inmates and they had spontaneously decided not to cooperate. The officer then wanted to know more about the general circumstances of the inmates in terms of food, health etc. I told him the whole truth: the anger about the suspension of buying food and receiving parcels, the poor quality of the prison food, the shortness of time in the courtyard in the fresh air, and the bitterness of the political prisoners that they were excluded from amnesties.

Two days later Wiese called me in. "Erler," he said, "you've done me a great favour." Whereas other *Saalälteste* gave the officers fairy tales about the prison - in order to suck up to the officials - I had been the only prisoner to tell them the truth. "And the officers believed only you." At this point Wiese became talkative. He told me about his own time as a Communist party member in a prison, which, under the Nazis, had been much harder than our time in Waldheim. After the liberation by the Russian troops, he had been forced by the Party to take on the job of prison director against his will. He tried, within the parameters of what was possible, to ensure a humane approach to imprisonment. I believed him.

I never heard of any mishandling of prisoners in Waldheim. Wiese did indeed take a humane approach with his prisoners. To give an example that I personally experienced: after I had been transferred from Bautzen to Waldheim I spent several weeks in solitary confinement. This was normal procedure in all DDR prisons for newcomers who would only be assigned to a hall after observation. Solitary confinement is a psychological and spiritual torture - at least it was for me. One day I totally lost control when a *Kalfaktor* brought me a piece of bread for breakfast that had evidently fallen into a coffee pot. I threw the wet bread back at him and screamed that he should eat it himself. I was still on a restricted diet because of my gastritis and symptoms of liver problems. A piece of bread like that would have soured my stomach. Naturally I did not get another piece of bread and had to do without breakfast that morning. But I was not punished. In previous prisons I would have been put in the bunker. Kommissar Wiese had - it appeared - an understanding for such "prison rage" when an inmate lost his nerves.

Much later, when I was in West Germany, I learned from a former inmate that Wiese had fled to the West shortly after the big prison release action in 1956, which also liberated me. However, Wiese had been sentenced to prison for two years in the West. If I had known about his trial, I would have come, even from overseas, to testify on his behalf. Even today, I feel deep misgivings about the fact that I was not in a position to help. I have no idea what became of him.

Release and Probationary Status

Khrushchev's speech against Stalin's terror at the 20th Party conference of the Communist Party of the Soviet Union in early 1956 was not published in the DDR but became known to people in the DDR, thanks to Western radio broadcasts. Khrushchev admitted that under Stalin millions of innocent people had been killed and that there were innocent political prisoners. This news reached us prison inmates. Finally Stalin, who had died two years earlier, was being recognised in his own land as a tyrant and a mass murderer. Could victims of the DDR-Stalinism like us now hope for release? We learned that the gates of Soviet labour camps and prisons had been opened for political prisoners. Inmates in the DDR who had been tried and condemned by Soviet military tribunals were now being released. Why were DDR-condemned prisoners not freed? Ulbricht, one of the most loyal Stalinists, showed no hurry in this respect. Under pressure from Soviet reformers, he finally began to release his political prisoners in May 1956.

About ten inmates from our hall had already been released when finally it was my turn. Kommissar Wiese gave me the happy news. He informed me that it was not an amnesty but rather release under parole. The 10-year probation period would include: upholding the confiscation of personal property (the inheritance from my mother) and stripping of my civil rights, including voting rights; also access to any leading position was forbidden. These details were of no interest to me. The important thing was to have the prison walls behind me and the possibility of fleeing to the West.

75

A week later I was transferred to a single-occupancy cell from which I was released the next day, on 16 June 1956. I will never forget the moment I was led across the courtyard of the prison and my fellow inmates cheered me from the open windows and yelled good wishes for my future. Few were given such a send off and certainly no other *Saalältester*! Nearly all the *Kapos* kowtowed to the prison guards and were distrusted and hated by inmates.

The clothes I had worn five years before fit me well enough - except for the trousers which I had to hold up with a belt made of string since I had lost so much weight. I was given a small amount of money so that I could buy a train ticket to Dresden. When I asked if I could have the money from my savings account, the salary from my work as payroll bookkeeper during my time in the Yellow Misery of Bautzen, I was told this would be transferred to me at a future date. I am still waiting for it today.

Once on the train, a talkative man sat down in my compartment. I distrusted him instinctively, thinking he was very likely from the Stasi who wanted to find out about me. Naturally I mentioned nothing of my plan to escape to the West as soon as possible. I said I was going to look for work to support the DDR. I ignored the politically charged comments that this *agent provocateur* produced. I returned directly home. The reunion with my father was touching. I was finally with a person I could fully trust.

After release from prison in June 1956, I weighed 158 lbs. and was 6 ft 4 inches tall.

The next day when I reported as required to the resident's registra-

tion office in Dresden I was told about not only the probation-
ary restrictions I knew all too well, but was also informed of
travel constraints. I was only allowed to travel within a radius
of 30 km of Dresden. Another obligation was to report regularly to this same bureau. Fortunately our weekend cottage in
Falkenhain (the Soviets and the East German regime allowed
the personal possession of a *Dacha*, a weekend house) lay within the 30 km limit so I could go there to rest a few days.

This first phase of my newly acquired freedom was harder for
me than the last years of prison. I never felt secure because I suspected everyone I met of being a Stasi spy, especially on public
transport. When someone criticised the system or praised me for
my "clean shirt" (it was generally known that you could sell your
soul, so to speak, in order to prevent political prison), I avoided

My DDR identity card: the serial number indicates the restricted radius of free
movement.

any criticism of the DDR regime. At all costs I had to create the impression in the minds of the authorities that I regretted my pro-Western actions and that I wanted to stay in Dresden.

With this in mind I went looking for a job. My high school education and accounting knowledge from community college should have gotten me a good job but every time I mentioned the restrictions tied to my probation I was suddenly no longer considered for a bookkeeping post but instead for a job as a labourer. In the end I took up the offer of a position as an assistant depot worker because there were two weeks before the job started. By then I would be in a position to get to West Berlin.

Escape to West Berlin

A lucky happenstance aided me in my plans to escape. In Dresden news of my release got around. Barely a week had gone by since my release when my younger brother's pediatrician got in touch with me and offered me a ride to Berlin in his car. Of course I did not receive this information by phone or post, but via a letter brought to our house by a trusted messenger. I agreed immediately but requested that we travel at a time when controls would be less strictly enforced. The doctor suggested we leave at about three in the morning so that I could take public transport during the peak travel period from Königswusterhausen, a suburb in the East of Berlin, via East Berlin to the Western Sector. In 1956 there was no Berlin Wall and free travel was still possible between East Germany and the Western Sectors of Berlin.

Just to be on the safe side, I sent an application for admission to Humboldt University in East Berlin and kept a copy of the letter in case we were stopped. I left a note for my father in our apartment telling him I was leaving. He knew this already, but we did not want the authorities to accuse him of complicity. Invoking liability of family members for the crimes of another member was a well-known practice by the Stasi. The letter I wrote was done to keep him out of their grips.

The 30 June 1956 was our date to meet on a street corner in the Southern suburb of Dresden. To avoid being detected, I did not turn on any lights in the flat and left the house by a back route across a neighbouring piece of land full of rubble from the bombings. The trip by car went smoothly but my driver, the doctor, had to stop twice because I was so nervous that I got a bad case of diarrhea. No wonder: if I had been caught I would have landed behind prison walls again for breaking probation. I travelled with a new DDR identity card that had been issued in Dresden. The serial number on it indicated the travel restrictions placed on me, but an uninitiated person would not know that. Travelling beyond the 30 km radius from Dresden was high risk, but at night and by road was the best option.

In Königswusterhausen, just outside the Berlin city limit, I got out of the car and bought a ticket on the S-Bahn to travel into the city. The underground and the S-Bahn had unrestricted lines all over Berlin without hindrance. Controls took place principally at the edge of the city limits, in my case in Königswusterhausen, not within the city itself.

The S-Bahn was chockablock full of people due to the morning rush hour. The police were satisfied with a glance of my identity card at a distance. They were interested in catching refugees from Poland without a DDR identity card. The rebellion in the Polish town of Posen had just taken place, and many Poles were on the run to the West. Thankfully there were no further controls on the train before the inner city sectors. So it was that I got off the train in Berlin-Wilmersdorf. In tears I hugged the first Western policeman I saw dressed in the traditional *Tschako* (a black headgear). For the first time in years I felt unfettered, really free. I could shrug off an incredibly heavy burden!

My older brother no longer lived in West Berlin. He had emigrated from West Berlin to Canada and I had no addresses of friends or acquaintances in West Berlin. I had to make my way to an address given to me by a refugee reception office. I received a CARE package (Cooperative for American Remittances to Europe), an American goodwill action after WW II. It contained the most essential items for daily life. My sole personal possessions were my school diplomas and my CV.

The interrogation I received from the Western security officials was very interesting. They knew all about me and welcomed me. They said that I was the only *Saalälteste* who had not become a spy for, or collaborator with, the prison guards. They thanked me for having helped so many fellow inmates endure their hard life.

The Americans offered me a payment of 200 Marks a month plus study costs, and reimbursement of all hospitality expenses, to report back to them about persons and groups at the university of my choice. I immediately rejected this proposal: I wanted to sleep with a clear conscience. I never ever wanted to act as an informer again. And I have never regretted this decision. Later, at Heidelberg University I met a student who had let himself be persuaded by the Americans. He invited me to generous meals and drinks in restaurants and paid for everything. Nevertheless he did not seem to have any friends.

Getting a flight out of West Berlin to West Germany took nearly four weeks. During this time I was able to meet up with my younger brother in West Berlin who was a student at the university in Jena. Although he was, like myself, the son of a "capitalist", he had been allowed to study in East Germany. He had told a classmate whose father was a high-ranking Stasi official that after completing secondary school he was going to go to the West. This was before the erection of the Berlin wall and was not yet illegal. There would have been no way he would have been admitted to a university in the DDR. The classmate must have discussed this potential brain drain from the DDR with his father because against all expectations, my brother was admitted to university.

During this time I also met my former classmate Helmut Otto, who had finished secondary school in West Berlin and was now studying at the *Freie Universität*. He was the person who took the blame for the Stalin telegram at school. My visit with the Freedom Lawyers didn't give me more information than I already knew. They confirmed that Dr Crusius who my father hired as my defense lawyer, had given them all the information about my case and that he now lived in the West.

SINCE 1956

IN THE WEST

Flight to West Germany: Student Years

On 28 July 1956 I was finally flown out through the allied air corridor from West Berlin to Frankfurt am Main. West Berlin was an island surrounded by the DDR, only an air corridor between West Berlin and West Germany guaranteed free and unrestricted travel. I was told to take a local train from Frankfurt to a refugee camp near Ulm and to report there. Still not fully free! From Ulm I telephoned the government in Stuttgart and got immediate permission to leave the camp. I went to the home of my good friend from school days in Altenberg, Peter Reinhold, who had finished his law studies in Heidelberg and was doing his legal training. I received a warm welcome from him and his quietly gracious mother. I stayed with them for the next six weeks. I spent most of that time travelling and having a recuperation stay in the Black Forest, prescribed by the Health Ministry.

Before I could think about studies at Heidelberg University, I had to find a way to support myself. I went to a string of offices where I had to fill in a great number of forms. There is a saying "Formulare von der Wiege bis zur Bahre" (forms from cradle to coffin). A bursary for my studies, modest social services subsidy, and regular State support as a former political prisoner finally enabled me to move into a student residence, the Collegium Academicum in Heidelberg.

After reading the catalogue of university courses intently, I finally enrolled in the Faculty of Law with a Minor in Economics. The study of Law included some History and Philosophy, and allowed me to attend lectures by famous professors in

85

Philosophy, Psychology and Art History. My *studium generale* was intended to help close the gaps in the knowledge base that I had brought from the East.

The *Allgemeiner Studentenausschuss* (Student Council) of the university offered me a position where I would be responsible for *Gesamtdeutsche Fragen* (All German Affairs), issues concerning refugees from the East. I soon became active in this role. Following the 1956 defeat of the Hungarian revolt in late autumn, I organised a spontaneous collection of money for the Hungarian refugee students. In four days volunteers collected 8,240 DM in and around the university - an impressive amount at the time.

A few days later when I met up with the Hungarian students who had made it to Heidelberg, I was impressed by their political views. They had demonstrated for freedom of expression, religion and travel, not against the socialistic economic system, which we Germans called "Goulash-Communism" because it was not as radical and orthodox as the DDR regime.

Aside from my work with the Student Council, I stayed away from all political activity. I did not join a political party, a fraternity or a club. Neither did I want to get engaged or married. I wanted to be unencumbered and free! It was only as a part-time freelance journalist that I took on political topics. I studied for two semesters in Switzerland and in this time the *Tribune de Lausanne* published on their front page a series of articles written by me in French entitled "The Position of Students in East Germany", "Living Conditions of Bautzen II Inmates" and "Political Trials and the Penitentiary in the German Democratic Republic". As an occasional freelance journalist, I wrote articles for the *Rhein-Neckar Zeitung, Heidelberger Tageblatt, and Mittelbayerische Zeitung* (Regensburg), but they, as well as all my subsequent publications have been travel reports and items of cultural interest. "Politics is a whore," said Goethe and I stayed well away from it.

Why then this political memoir? An ego trip? Perhaps. In any case I want it to stand as my contribution toward understanding and putting to rest the history of the DDR. *Sine ira et studio*, without anger and zealotry. I tried to write objective *Erlebte Zeitgeschichte* (contemporary history I went through).

By abstaining from politics I could gradually push aside the terrible memories of prison in my head. This took years - decades in fact. I had nightmares of interrogation scenes from which I would wake to the sound of my own screams of fear and bathed in sweat. But later this gave way to less troubled sleep.

Hilfskomitee für politische Häftlinge
der Sowjetzone

Durch die zuständige Finanzbehörde als besonders
förderungswürdige gemeinnützige Organisation
anerkannt. Spenden sind steuerbegünstigt)

Geschäftsführung: Untersuchungsausschuß Freiheitlicher Juristen
Telefon: 84 30 61, Apparat 49 / Postscheckkonto: Berlin-West 499 99

Berlin-Zehlendorf-West, den 10.7.56 Kr.
Limastraße 30 r

B e s c h e i n i g u n g

Herr Jochen E r l e r , geb. am 29.3.1932 in Dresden, vor seiner
Verhaftung wohnhaft gewesen in Dresden, Bayreutherstr. 32, z.Zt.
ansässig in Berlin-Kreuzberg, Bärwaldstr. 5 b. Wolf, ist wegen seiner ehrenamtlichen Mitarbeit beim Untersuchungsausschuß freiheitlicher Juristen (von Dezember 1949 bis zur Verhaftung im Jahre 1951)
am 2.8.1951 durch den SSD in Dresden auf dem Bahnhof verhaftet und
am 2o.12.1951 durch das Landgericht Dresden nach Art. 6 in Verbindung mit KD 38 II III A III zu 6 Jahren Zuchthaus und den oblig.
Sühnemaßnahmen verurteilt worden.

Herr Erler hat von der gegen ihn verhängten Strafe fast 5 Jahre in
Bautzen und Waldheim verbüßt. Im Zuge einer Entlassungsaktion wurde
er vorzeitig, mit bedingter Strafaussetzung, am 15.6.1956 aus Waldheim entlassen.

Herr Erler ist dem UFJ als aufrechter, ehrenhafter Charakter bekannt. Seine Mitarbeit war für den UFJ eine wertvolle Hilfe im Kampf
gegen das Unrechtssystem der SBZ. Seine Verurteilung steht im Wider-
spruch zu rechtsstaatlichen Grundsätzen und somit sind die Folgen
von dem Betroffenen auch nicht selbst zu vertreten.

Nach unserem Dafürhalten müßten die Bestimmungen des HHG vom 6.8.55
auf Herrn Erler voll Anwendung finden, zumal Ausschließungsgründe
hier nicht bekannt sind.

Belastendes ist ebenfalls in unseren Karteien nicht verzeichnet.

HILFSKOMITEE (Kreuzer)
FÜR POLITISCHE HÄFTLINGE
Postscheckkonto Berlin-West Nr. 499 99

88

ASSISTANCE COMMITTEE FOR POLITICAL PRISONERS OF THE SOVIET ZONE

Berlin 10.7.56

To whom it may concern

Mr Jochen Erler, born 29.3.1932 in Dresden, prior resident of Dresden at Bayretherstr. 32, presently residing in Berlin-Kreuzberg at 5b Bärwaldstr. was arrested by the SSD on 2.8.1951 at the train station in Dresden because of his voluntary collaboration with the Investigations Committee of Free Lawyers (UFJ). He was sentenced by the district court of Dresden on 20.12.1951 to 6 years penitentiary in accordance to Art.6 of KD 38 II III A IIII.

Mr Erler was held for 5 years in Bautzen and Waldheim. On 15.6.1956, following a release campaign, he was released early from the Waldheim penitentiary under conditional suspension of sentence.

Mr Erler is known to the UFJ as an honourable person of integrity. His collaboration with the UFJ constituted a valuable contribution in the fight of the West against the regime of injustice in the SBZ. As his condemnation contradicts the rules of law, the consequences of the Court's sentence are not his responsibility.

It is our opinion that the provisions of the HHG from 6.8.55 should be fully applied to Mr Erler, particularly as we know no reasons for exclusion.

Furthermore, our files do not contain any incriminating evidence.

Translation. This attestation, as well as a similar text that I had received from the International League of Human Rights, were helpful in my dealings with city and state authorities, and supported my applications for grants and scholarships at universities.

89

Shadows of My Past: Second-Class Citizen?

After graduating from University of Heidelberg with a Bachelors Degree in Law, the 1st *Staatsexamen*, I accepted a post-graduate scholarship to McGill University in Montreal where I obtained a Masters of Law. From there I returned to Heidelberg and acquired a Doctorate in International Law. After two years of legal training in Germany I passed the 2nd *Staatsexamen*, my admission to Bar and Bench, in Munich. Instead of an assignment as a judge in the Bavarian Forest, a role that was offered to me, I opted for international work and applied for a diplomatic job at the Foreign Ministry in order to work abroad. I had gained a taste for the wider world. Several Scholarships from DAAD (the German student exchange program) and grants had funded my studies at universities in Lausanne and Montreal, the International Court of Justice in The Hague, the UN in Geneva, attendance of conferences in Calgary, Dallas and Durham, and especially an internship at the UN.

"Erler has ants in his pants" a primary school teacher had said of me years and years before. Travel restrictions on DDR citizens, and especially the years in prison, had made those ants even busier. However, my application to the Foreign Ministry revealed the disadvantage of my East German background: it was a liability. My job interview began on a promising note, but having close relations in the DDR meant that for security reasons I could not be considered for employment in the diplomatic service. This was very disappointing although I could understand their recruitment policy. My younger brother worked as a psychologist at the Dresden Hygiene Museum.

The UN Interns of 1963: I am the fourth from the left in the last row. In mid 1963, when Germany was not yet a member of the UN, I was was the first ever German national at the UN Headquarters. I completed my practicum in the Legal Office.

At a reception for the interns by the UN Secretary General, U Thant

The Convocation Ceremony for a Master of Laws (LL.M.) at McGill University in Montréal

The Stasi could put pressure on him in order to recruit me as a spy (this happened anyhow, much later).

Fortunately such security risks did not enter into procedures when I applied for a job at the World Campus Afloat, part of *Chapman College* in California. I was recruited as a lecturer for one semester for a cruise halfway around the world, lecturing on International Studies, the second semester as Associate Professor.

"Publish or perish" was the by-word in US academia. I enjoyed lecturing but had spent

As Dr jur. during my legal training in Regensburg in 1966

more than enough time in university libraries, particularly as a doctoral student and as the Research Assistant to a professor in Montreal for whom I had worked for many years. I hoped I could rest on the laurels of my long list of academic publications. But this was not granted me. The College expected me to continue to research and publish academic articles. I was just not interested, so I looked around for a new employment.

The Slippery Slope of Diplomacy

As a substitute for my frustrated career hopes as a diplomat in the German Foreign Ministry, I considered working as an international civil servant in the UN Development Programme. (UNDP). The German Federal Republic, although not yet a member of the UN, nevertheless made considerable contributions to the Special Fund and to Technical Assistance which were part of UNDP. On that basis I could apply for a job there.

From Bonn, the adminstrative capital of West Germany, I received the necessary *clearance* regarding my personal integrity which international organisations request from the applicant's national government. I was recruited by UNDP as their *Agreements Officer* to look at the legal aspects of all the Technical Assistance, Special Fund and Headquarters Agreements made between the UN and the developing countries.

Security aspects which had apparently troubled the German Foreign Ministry did not play the same role here since the Soviet Union and its satellite countries were members of the UN. Moreover there were and still are scarcely any secrets in multinational organisations.

Nevertheless I had not forgotten my job interview in Bonn. It made me more politically alert. I was aware of political traps. As a bureaucrat at UN Headquarters in New York from 1968 and later in the field, I avoided all unnecessary contact with colleagues from Eastern Europe and their diplomatic representatives. It was widely known that the frequent cocktail parties, personal invitations to dinner or cultural events and even study trips to the Soviet Union in Aeroflot jets were used to recruit

UN Headquarters and in the background the United Nations Development
Programme (UNDP) in the Alcoa Building: I worked here over several years between
1968 and 1976.

In front of the UN Headquarters, New York, NY

spies. I stayed well away from all, together with my wife Lynn from Pacific Palisades/Los Angeles, married since 1968.

I learned later from a colleague who worked in Technical Assistance in a West African country how the Soviets had developed files on all international experts and members of international organisations. Any international civil servant was a potential candidate to become a spy for the Russians, either through blackmailing or convincing. My colleague had been shown his file by a friendly Russian in Nigeria after they had gone on a drinking spree together. The file had details of his family, his work life, his career so far and his weakness for alcohol. My colleague saw notes about his various adulterous encounters during a previous field assignment. The Russian bragged that he had a file on every UN employee and every co-worker of every aid organisation in Nigeria. As I have already stated, I was not interested in providing additional data for the files on me by the Soviets in New York. I wanted to appear as inauspicious and as uninteresting as possible to them.

In my function as UNDP's "Agreements Officer", I am presenting documents for signature to Paul Hoffmann, Administrator of UNDP, and the Ambassador of New Zealand.

Travels Behind the Iron Curtain

In 1977 I was sent to Poland on official travel for UNDP. I seised this opportunity to make a family trip and a stopover in Dresden to see my father and my younger brother Frido. Since the trip was protected by diplomatic status, I was safe from possible arrest for breaking the conditions of my bail. For the purpose of getting a visa, and not reveal Dresden as my place of birth, I handed in my UN Laissez-Passer to the DDR observer mission at the UN and not my West German passport. I was the first and the last German to get a DDR visa in the UN Laissez-Passer, because the East Germans later would not accept the UN Laissez-Passer when granting a visa.

The trip took place without incident. As envoy of the UN I was treated everywhere with friendly courtesy. Walter Ulbricht had been replaced by Erich Honecker in 1971 as First Secretary of the Central Committee and as chairman of the State's National Defence Council. In 1972 Chancellor Willy Brandt had opened up dialogue with the DDR by means of a Treaty and the DDR had gained self-confidence on the international stage. Political jokes were generally tolerated and no longer rewarded with imprisonment. A policeman who knew my background said to me, "Hats off. You had the courage to live according to your convictions. Others and I have been collaborators."

Nevertheless citizens were still subjected to State-supplied indoctrination. Every measure was taken to stop radio and television access to broadcasts from the West. In 1961, the Berlin Wall had been erected and the border between East and West Germany was closed. Permits for travel to the West were only

UNITED NATIONS
NATIONS UNIES

82274

DESCRIPTION OF BEARER
SIGNALEMENT DU PORTIER
ПРИМЕТЫ ПРЕДЪЯВИТЕЛЯ
DESCRIPCIÓN DEL PORTADOR

HAIR:
CHEVEUX: BROWN – CHATAINS
ЦВЕТ ВОЛОС:
CABELLO:

HEIGHT:
TAILLE: 6 Ft. 1 – 1M 85 1/2
РОСТ:
ESTATURA:

DATE OF BIRTH:
DATE DE NAISSANCE: 29 MARCH 1932
ДАТА РОЖДЕНИЯ:
FECHA DE NACIMIENTO:

EYES: BLUE – BLEUS
YEUX:
ЦВЕТ ГЛАЗ:
OJOS:

DISTINGUISHING MARKS OR FEATURES:
SIGNES PARTICULIERS:
ОСОБЫЕ ПРИМЕТЫ:
SEÑAS PARTICULARES:

VISAS

Deutsche Demokratische Republik
Den Deutschland
02.09.1977

Ausreiseberechtigung
für die
Deutsche Demokratische Republik
den Deutschland
gültig bis 07.09.1977

Deutsche Demokratische Republik

Deutsche Demokratische Republik

Visum Nr. 80/398
zur Einreise
und Ausreise (ein - zwei - malig)
vom 15. August 1977
bis 04. Sept. 1977
nach Dresden
für alle staatlichen Grenzübergangsstellen
Washington, D.C. 0 1 UN 41

My UN Laissez-Passer Passport that contained the Visa from the DDR

99

given to pensioners, to young people loyal to the Stasi, and to some eminent personalities in culture and science. Moving to the West was practically impossible even for the purpose of family reunion. Writers and other artists had to be pro-regime. Dire punishments meted out for fleeing the country or aiding in such attempts! It was no wonder that I protected myself with diplomatic immunity, kept vigilant and engaged in no political discussion.

I could not combine my second journey into the *Paradies der Werktätigen* (Paradise of the Workers), the East German self-description of their State, with a similar official function. Fortunately there was no need to do so. I had made enquiries regarding such a trip at the Ministry for Pan-German issues and they had swept aside my concerns and doubts about safety. Since the Treaty made by Chancellor Brandt and Erich Honecker, and a DDR amnesty for East German fugitives, there had been no further arrests of former DDR citizens when on a visit to the DDR.

And indeed: this trip was with only two minor incidents. When crossing the border on our way (I travelled again with my wife and children) into the DDR, the border-police confiscated a book and a calendar that I had brought along as presents. The calendar showed classic cars, and as such had no political meaning. However, the 17 June, the day of the anti-communist uprising in 1953, was marked as a national holiday and this was offensive to the official. The book was about the early history of air balloons with reproductions of old prints and drawings. This was confiscated because a few days earlier some East Germans had escaped to the West using an air balloon. Apparently the guards thought the book could incite people to flee to the West this way.

Once in Dresden, we had to register as visitors to the city. At the registration office I was approached by an official and

With my father who visited me in the West

invited to a chat in a restaurant to discuss preserving world peace. Were we not all against war and for peace and understanding between peoples? Very politely I refused the invitation. My time was limited and did not allow for it, and especially such a "chat" was for the purpose of winning over collaborators. My friend Peter Reinhold, for instance, had been approached on one of his trips to Dresden to have one such "chat". Peter was asked to set up a dead letter box, a secret location to deposit messages. Later they would have asked him to do more serious work. Obviously, they approached the wrong person. He would have never done that!

Under Suspicion of Being a Spy

Despite all efforts to keep my contact with the East to a minimum and my determination to abstain from any political activity, the burden of my DDR past once again came to play in my professional life.

After ten years (1968-1979) working for the UN in New York and in Haiti, I had left the UN and obtained employment with a better salary at OECD (Organisation for Economic Cooperation and Development) in Paris from 1979-1984. I had fulfilled all requirements as an international civil servant and had been successful for four years in my work, but was denied a permanent contract which at the time could be expected. Something was wrong; there was an obstacle for my career I could not detect. My bosses invented reasons for denying me a permanent contract, reasons I could easily counter. During almost five years of intensive work I had gained the full confidence and trust of my Section. We were happy in Paris. My wife Lynn worked as a teacher and the children had finally integrated in the French environment.

Worried about my job and frustrated in my work I looked elsewhere for employment. A similar position to the one I had at OECD opened up in England at the European Centre for Medium-range Weather Forcasts (ECMWF) in Reading, a town between London and Oxford. I applied successfully for the job, and worked there from 1984 - 1989 until retirement.

In England, at ECMWF, my section comprised of 12 staff members, in contrast to the 30 staff at OECD. In Paris I had been responsible for administration of a personnel of 1500, and several hundred pensioned staff, whereas now I was only in charge of 150 altogether. On the plus side, the salary was the same, and thanks to my reduced responsibilities and reduced exposure to internal power struggles, I had a much easier job than before.

My problem at OECD revealed itself several months into my new post when I received a letter from the German Embassy in London. The Office of the West German State Prosecutor at the Federal Court of Justice in Karlsruhe called me as a witness against my oldest friend Fritz Oschatz who had been arrested and indicted as an Eastern spy. But in reality I was assumed to have been a collaborator of Fritz.

This explained why I was considered a security risk for OECD. Mr Berline in charge of security at OECD had no other option than to block the grant of a permanent contract . Now I understood why my telephone at OECD had been tapped. A friend at the switchboard had told me about this, but in my naivety I thought it might have been a normal procedure in the interest of security. I understood why an American of Greek origin who had been seconded from the State Department to OECD, had shown so much personal interest in me. Evidently he was a collaborator of the American Secret Service. He had told me several pieces of misinformation in order, I assume, to track their spread to secret agents in the East.

The Case of Fritz Oschatz

The interrogation session at the German Embassy in London was extremely interesting. Right at the start I asked the official from Pullach, Headquarters of West Germany's Secret Service near Munich, why there was such interest in my childhood friend. He told me that Fritz was a Major in the Red Army and that he had already received two high decorations from the Su-

Photo of Fritz Oschatz, my friend who was a spy.

preme Soviet authorities. My interrogator also mentioned that before being put in charge of Fritz Oschatz's case, he had handled the Guillaume case (the spy in Willy Brandt's chancellor's office). In other words he only dealt with top spies. According to him, Fritz had been the most effective military spy for the Russians in West Germany. Then he asked me about my relationship with Fritz.

I recounted how Fritz had been my best friend from primary school in Dresden. At that time our family lived in Reichenbach Street and Fritz and his mother lived around the corner in Uhland Street. His mother ran a laundry service that my parents used. Fritz's father, an old communist, had disappeared. Either he had gone to the Soviet Union or had been sent by the Nazis to a concentration camp. My father, who since the persecution of the Jews and the introduction of the Hitler greeting could no longer stand the Nazis and who had been thrown out of the Party for his negative views on Nazi politics, took Fritz under his wing. Fritz was often invited on outings to our weekend cottage and also to our home in Dresden.

Together in *Fähnlein 53* of the *Hitlerjugend* (Hitler's youth organisation) Fritz and I carried out our obligations. Fritz appeared to like and enjoy the sport exercises, games and *Sternfahrten* (excursions), unlike myself, and became my *Jungenschaftsführer* (group leader). In any case, as often as I could, I skipped the meetings.

After the Dresden bombings, Fritz and I met again in Dresden. Fritz lived together with his partner Renate, whom he married quite some time later. We spent many weekends together in our cottage in the Erzgebirge mountains in Falkenhain, with the motto of "wine, women and song".

When I was living in the West after my escape from the DDR, Fritz got in touch with me. He was also now a refugee having left Dresden before the Wall was built. At his request I wrote a statement for him that he needed to be acknowledged as a refugee in the Federal Republic of Germany. I declared that to my knowledge Fritz had in no way engaged in political or spy activities.

When I went to Canada for two years of post-graduate studies, I asked Fritz to send parcels every month to my father in Dresden. This was allowed from within West Germany but not from abroad. Fritz was happy to take on this task. After I had finished my training in Germany, when I was again planning to go abroad Fritz offered again to send the parcels. I was very happy with this because for my father, a pensioner in a Dresden, these parcels were a great help. The goods we could send like coffee, raisins, chocolate etc. were only available in the *Intershops* against payment in Westmarks, and customers were Western visitors and highly placed local officials. Normal DDR citizens were not allowed to have West German money. It was only later that the West Mark became a second DDR currency and the possession of Western currency was no longer against the law.

105

Fritz and Renate had continued over many years to send parcels to my father. And this was the key point for the security police officials: Fritz had used the food packets to send the results of his spy activity to the East. Stasi officials or the Russians opened every packet that arrived from the West at the post office for the purposes of control. Often the officials took articles for themselves, but my father had written to me that from a certain point in time no further items had been stolen. No wonder - those Stasi or Russian officials (until the fall of communism in 1989, Putin was in charge of the operations in Dresden) who were opening the packets to my father had more important things to look for!

Fritz and Renate had started their life in the West in Bamberg, where they had established contacts with US Army officers in the German-American Club, but also in Heidelberg where the American Occupation Army had Headquarters. I had introduced Fritz and Renate to the mother of another old friend from Dresden, who was the vice-president of the German-American Club in Heidelberg. Fritz was trained in technical drawing and employed at Teldix Company in Heidelberg as an engineer responsible for packaging. This company was producing electronics for the Starfighter airplane to be delivered to the West German Airforce. And the Federal Republic lost a large number of these airplanes, all due to unexplained technical failure! Elsewhere the Starfighter had no such problems. Had Fritz interfered with the enclosed instructions at some point, or did he have a collaborator at Teldix?

Be that as it may, the security official told me that they had been shadowing Fritz and me for a long while, at least two years. Fritz had been very careful in his activities and had only once been observed using a dead letter box near Cologne. I could confirm that Fritz had often travelled to Cologne where he purportedly had relatives. I learned from the official that it was there that Fritz had contact with members of the Soviet Military Attaché.

The interrogating official asked me whether I wanted to lodge a criminal charge against Fritz for his possible role in shadowing me and for my arrest in East Germany. I told him I thought it would be impossible to prove this. I also hoped that our friendship would have been too important to Fritz to denounce me.

There were now two facts that indicated that Fritz had good contacts to the Russians. How else could it be explained that after my arrest the usual search through our house had not taken place? Such a search would have endangered my father, who had items and goods still in storage there. I think that Fritz prevented a house search by the Stasi to protect my father.

The rather correct treatment that I had experienced during interrogation by the Russian officer was in total contrast to what fellow inmates suffered when interrogated by Russians. This also led me to assume that Fritz had influenced his Russian colleagues

Thinking back to our drinking bouts in Falkenhain, I wonder whether Fritz was already observing me in his role as a Soviet secret police collaborator. He and Renate insisted on photographing each other naked after playing the dice game *Entblättere das Bäumchen* (strip the tree of its leaves). I only took pictures of Renate, not of us men. Compromising pictures taken in hotel rooms with hidden cameras was one way secret services in East Bloc countries blackmailed people and recruited agents.

I asked the interrogating security officer to keep me informed about the case. A few months later, shortly before the Berlin Wall had come down, he informed me that Fritz had been sentenced to two years' imprisonment, and that after his appeal, he was released on bail and disappeared to the East. It is a pity because I would have liked to learn more from Fritz about our common past and his spying activities.

After that interrogation in London I reflected on the death of Renate, the wife of Fritz. Around 1984, shortly before the detection of Fritz as a spy for the East, I had been again in Heidelberg and visited Fritz. He was there without Renate - she had died in a car accident. One of the front wheels had come off the car and she had run into a wall. My question was: who loosened the bolts on the wheel? Was it the Soviet Secret Service, or a Western secret service? Had Renate become an inconvenient partner of Fritz, a liabilty? Was it a warning signal? In any case, Fritz did nothing vis-à-vis the auto repair company that had the car for service a few days prior to the accident. Why not?

My Second Rehabilitation

I have to admit that my surveillance by the Western secret services was justified - Fritz had after all made use of my family and of my name to send the products of his spying activities to the East Bloc. I am nevertheless deeply hurt given my active resistance to the Stalinist regime and as a survivor of the Yellow Misery. The two years I was under surveillance by Western secret services could have been carried out without destroying my successful and very promising career with the OECD.

If there had been proof I was a spy, the OECD could have fired me at any time. As there was no proof at all, the withholding of a proper regularisation of my contractual situation at OECD should have been explained to me. But neither the German Government nor the OECD offered a word of regret or any support toward me after I had been cleared. I was in a very fragile situation, an international civil servant with only a short-term contract.

In order to safeguard myself for the years to come, I requested a security check. I knew that I had nothing to hide, that I had a "clean shirt". I eventually got the Ministry of Transport in Bonn, in charge of liaison with ECMWF, to initiate the procedure. More than a year later I was told that my NATO security classification was *Cosmic*, the highest level of clearance one can get. But a great number of friends and professional acquaintances who were interrogated have never been informed about my clearance. This may explain the loss of contact with some of my old friends.

After my escape to the West I had already been rehabilitated by the West German authorities with regard to my trial and condemnation in 1951. The new "clearance" was in effect my second rehabilitation.

And since then I have been free of the shadows of my past (at least I think so).

EPILOGUE

Seeing My Stasi Files

I watched the fall of the Berlin Wall on television with Detlef Gebauer, a schoolfriend, at his house in Mühlacker. He had also been in prison for political reasons, but only for a short time, and had coincidentally passed through the same cell in the Schießgasse at Dresden's prison where I had been prior to my trial. He found the name Rano scratched onto the cell wall. Rano was my nickname in secondary school but the prison guards did not know that. If they had known I had scratched my name on the wall, they would have sent me to the bunker.

After escaping to the West, Detlef had become active in local politics in Mühlacker. Detlef was a surgeon and the medical advisor for an important soccer team in southern Germany. He travelled from time to time into the DDR after the signing of the *Ostverträge*, the treaty for coexistence between East and West Germany signed by Brandt and Honecker. After the *Wende*, the fall of the Berlin Wall and the Communist regime in East Germany, Detlef chose suicide after having been told he was required to report to an interrogation by the police. Had incriminating material been found in his Stasi files when after the collapse of the DDR, the West German security services sifted through the Stasi files to identify former Stasi collaborators and prevent that they would keep their public functions? This incident like the dubious car accident that killed Renate raised questions for me.

I will never know.

A family-visit to Dresden offered the opportunity to look at my Stasi files and also those of my late brother Frido. My file was virtually empty although it must have been quite fat by 1951. A friend had informed me back then that my file was a thick one and suggested that I better leave for the West. What was now shown to me 40 years later contained only a few pieces of paper. The Stasi stated (my translation) "Erler, Jochen, as was known through an informer, has links with the Investigatory Committee of the Lawyers for Freedom in West Berlin and travels in irregular intervals to West Berlin in order to bring to them information collected here. He has a wide circle of acquaintances. These persons are largely part of the LDP, some of whom study at the FU (*Freie Universität* in West Berlin). We do not know to what extent he gets his information from his circle of acquaintances. The informer is part of this process."

I am sure that most of the contents of my file were destroyed during the last days of the DDR, to protect Fritz Oschatz.

On another sheet I found the following text (my translation): "This Jochen is to be watched secretly and on a trip to Berlin by train from Dresden is to be arrested and interrogated. If he honestly reveals all, immediately place him under probation. Inform his friend as soon as the arrest is made." The "friend" in question was either Eberhard Fuchs or Günther Hastenrath who had denounced me. The order for arrest was dated 2 August 1951, the day of my arrest.

The file of my brother Frido was, in contrast, quite full. As an Official of the Dresden Health Museum he was under considerable pressure from the SED. Shortly before the fall of the Berlin wall he had joined the Party whereupon he received the order to recruit me as a spy. At that time I was working in Paris at the OECD where the strategically important International Energy Agency (IEA), a US initative, has its Headquarters. As I learned much later, a spy for the East had been detected at IEA around this time; hence the DDR's sudden interest in me to replace him I learned from the file that between 1981 and 1982 Frido had

With my brothers at a meeting in West Berlin before the wall had been built: my older brother Klaus on a visit from Canada, my younger brother Frido still a student in the DDR

to attend eight *conspiracy meetings* (as they were called in the Stasi file) with Stasi personnel and to report the political stances of his colleagues at work. He presented them all as pro-DDR, neither listened to nor watched Western radio or television, nor did tell political jokes. An annotation indicated that Frido was not entirely to be believed. He was described as "very reluctant" with regard to giving information about his colleagues. Hence Frido's request to be permitted travel to the West as *Reisekader* (a reliable official who is expected to return to the East) was rejected. The Stasi also stepped back from obliging him to become a collaborator.

When I was finished looking at the files and was preparing to leave, an official brought me another file. "Ernst Baum" was written on the cover and the official explained that it was a covert name the Stasi had invented for me. There were only two pages in this file. The working document was dated 1984 when I was in my last months of work at OECD. The only entry aside from my address was "Employee at OECD in Paris". The closing report from January 1988 noted that I was not any longer employed at OECD. In any case I have to thank my brother Frido that he did not sell me to the Stasi and instead sacrificed a good position in the Dresden Hygiene Museum. He left life with a clean shirt, too early to experience the reunification of Germany.

Glossary and Abbreviations

Agent Provocateur: inciting agent

BBC: British Broadcasting Corporation

Boykotthetze: expressing a political opinion not in line with the communists, political jokes, possessing Western newspapers, any action that could be construed as propaganda against the DDR

Brownshirts: a popular term for the members of the Nazi Party wearing brown shirts

Brown Years: the years under the Nazis (the Bownshirts)

Bunker: a dark cell in the cellar of a prison for punishment

CARE: Cooperative for Assistance & Relief Everywhere (US)

Charité: famous medical hospital in Berlin

Chruschtschow: Nikita C., Soviet politician who in 1956 initiated the de-Stalinisation (alias Khrushchev)

DAAD: Deutscher Akademischer Austauschdienst, the equivalent of the American Fulbright scholarship program

Dacha: a seasonal or year-round second home in Russia

DDR: Deutsche Demokratische Republik, German Democratic Republic, the former SBZ (Sowjetische Besatzungszone) in the Eastern part of post-war Germany

DM: Deutsche Mark (former currency)

DP: Displaced Person; during WWII the Germans forced people of occupied territories to work in Germany

DSF: Gesellschaft für Deutsch-Sowjetische Freundschaft, Society for German-Soviet Friendship

D-Zug: Durchgangszug (fast long distance train)

ECMWF: European Centre for Medium-range Weather Forecasts

East Germany: this is the commonly used term for the "Eastern part of post-war Germany" which is "Mitteldeutschland", Central Germany; East Germany proper was lost in WWII

East Berlin: the Eastern sector of post-war Berlin (occupied by the Russians)

Eastmark: the currency in the SBZ/DDR

FDJ: Freie Deutsche Jugend, Free German Youth, the communist-leaning youth organisation in the Eastern part of post-war Germany

Freedom Lawyers: Investigation Committee of Freedom Lawyers (Untersuchungsausschuss Freiheitlicher Juristen), formerly East German lawyers in West Berlin collecting information about infringements of human rights in the East

Freie Universität: Freie Universität in West Berlin, created after the division of Berlin; the original University of Berlin, the Humboldt University, was located in East Berlin

Goulash-communism: colloquial term for the communist regime in Hungary

Gulag: forced-labour camp in the Soviet Union

Hakenkreuz: swastika

HHG: Haftlingshilfegesetz (statute for assistince for political prisoners)

HJ: Hitlerjugend, the youth organisation in Nazi Germany

HO: Handels Organisation (state-owned supermarket in DDR)

ICSC: International Civil Service Commission (UN)

Jungenschaft: the smallest Unit of the Hitlerjugend

KGB: USSR Committee for State Security, the Soviet Secret Service (alias NKWD)

Khrushchev: Nikita K., Soviet politician who in 1956 initiated the de-Stalinisation, alias Chruschtschow

Kapo: Inmate of a Concentration Camp in charge of some adminstrative duties

KPD: Kommunistische Partei Deutschlands, Communist Party of Germany, one of the political parties in post-war Germany

KPdSU: Kommunistische Partei der Sowjet Union

KR Direktive: Kontrollrats Direktive: a law made jointly by the four victorious powers intented to apply against Nazis

LDP: Liberal Demokratische Partei, Liberal Democratic Party, one of the political parties in post-war Germany (DDR)

Liga für Menschenrechte: League for Human Rights, West Berlin

Me109: the German WWII fighter plane designed by Messerschmitt

Messerschmitt: Germany's fighter plane in WWII

National Front: National Alignment of all the political parties in the SBZ/DDR

NAPOLA: Nationalpolitische Lehranstalt, were special schools for indoctrinating German youth with Nazi propaganda

Nazi: a popular term for a member of the Nazi Party

NF: National Front

NKWD: abbreviation for the Soviet Secret Service (alias KGB)

NSDAP: National Sozialistische Deutsche Arbeiter Partei (Hitler's Party)

OECD: Organisation for Economic Cooperation and Development

Ostbüro der SPD: the Office of the SPD in West Berlin mainly to support anti-communist activities in East Germany

Pieck: Wilhelm Pieck, the first President of the DDR

RIAS: Rundfunk im amerikanischen Sektor (West Berlin), Radio in the American Sector of Berlin

SA: Sturm Abteilung

Saalältester: a prisoner appointed by the Police to keep order in a hall of between 120 and 200 prisoners; called "Kapo" in the concentration camps during Hitler's time

S-Bahn: Schnellbahn, public transport on rails, fast local train

SBZ: Sowjetische Besatzungszone, Soviet Occupation Zone in the Eastern part of post-war Germany

SED: Sozialistische Einheitspartei Deutschlands, Socialist Unity Party of Germany, the communist-directed unified KPD and SPD in the SBZ and DDR

Soviet Union: the Union of Soviet Socialist Republics, USSR, 1922 - 1991

SPD: Sozialdemokratische Partei Deutschlands, Social Democratic Party of Germany, one of the political parties in post-war Germany

SSD: Staatssicherheitsdienst (Stasi)

Stachelschweine: porcupines; the name of a Cabaret in West Berlin

Stalin: Joseph Stalin, 1920 - 1953 leader of the Soviet Union

Stalinorgel: Stalin's organ, a popular term for Russia's rocket launcher in WWII, resembling a church organ, and creating a howling sound

Stasi: Staatssicherheitsdienst, State Security, the Secret Service of the DDR

T-34: the Russian tank in WWII

U-Boot: submarine/subway, here referring to the infamous former Gestapo underground torture cells in Berlin, also used by the Russian and East German Secret Services

U-Haft: Untersuchungshaft (custodial imprisonment)

UFJ: Untersuchungsausschuss Freiheitlicher Juristen, Investigations Committee of Freedom Lawyers (West Berlin)

UNDP: United Nations Development Programme

UNO: United Nations Organisation

USSR: Soviet Union

VEB: Volkseigener Betrieb, state-owned enterprise, mostly expropriated former private property

VVN: Vereinigung der Verfolgten des Naziregimes, Association of Victims of the Nazi Regime

West Berlin: the 3 Western sectors of post-war Berlin (American, English and French)

Westmark: the currency in the Western part of occupied Germany

Winterhilfswerk: Winter Relief of the German People, organised by the Nazis

WWII: World War II

Zeugen Jehovas: Jehovah's Witnesses, a religious group

Vita Jochen Erler

Born March 1932: son of the owner of Gardinen Erler, the leading 3-floor department store for interior decoration in Dresden/Saxony

1943: due to the evacuation of children to the countryside, sent with his older brother to a farm in Wendisch Baselitz/Lausitz

1944: conspirative collaboration with prisoners of war and deported persons; compulsory admission to a Nazi-run boarding school in Altenberg/Erzgebirge; his older brother was sent to a penal NAtionalPOLitische Anstalt (NAPOLA)

1945: parents lose home and business due to the bombing of Dresden; family moves to the weekend house in Falkenhain in the Erzgebirge mountains; Russian troops conquer Saxony; return to Dresden; admission to Dresden Plauen High School

1946: a few months in the boarding Hermann-Lietz-School in Haubinda/Thuringia

1949: political activity at school; establishing contact with the League for Human Rights and the Freedom Lawyers in West Berlin

1950: final exam at school, but no admission to university; employment in the Provincial Statistics Office in Dresden

1951: arrest by the Stasi; 16 weeks in investigative custody by the Russians and the Stasi; sentenced to 6 years penitentiary, confiscation of assets and 10 years sanctions

1951-56: detention in Gulag-like Bautzen prison and in Waldheim prison

1956: thanks to de-Stalinisation by Chruschtschow in the Soviet Union, conditional release from prison and escape to the West

1956-65: student in Heidelberg and Lausanne; postgraduate studies at McGill (LL.M.) and Heidelberg (Dr jur.)

1963: UN Intern Program (the first German national in the UN Secretariat)

1965-68: legal training in Regensburg (admission to the Bar & Bench); Research Assistant for Prof. Mateesco Matte (Montreal)

1968: guest Lecturer and 1974 Assistant Professor of International Studies at the World Campus Afloat (Chapman College, California)

1968-89: international civil service at UNDP, UN, ICSC, OECD and ECMWF

1983-85: under surveillance by the Secret Services of Germany, France and the US

1989-2013: residence in Oxford: tour leader for Wine Trails, Rambler Holidays and Waymark Holidays, wine writer, taster at international wine and spirits competitions, and wine lecturer at conferences and on cruise ships

Since 2013: residence in Austria: continuing wine activities.

www.ingramcontent.com/pod-product-compliance
Lightning Source LLC
Chambersburg PA
CBHW020509040426
42331CB00042BA/107